THE HISTORY OF EUROPE

From the Dark Ages to the Renaissance

700–1599AD

THE HISTORY OF EUROPE

From the Dark Ages to the Renaissance

700–1599AD

MITCHELL BEAZLEY

From the Dark Ages to the Renaissance

Published in 2006 by Mitchell Beazley,
an imprint of Octopus Publishing Group Ltd
2–4 Heron Quays, London E14 4JP
Copyright © Octopus Publishing Group Ltd 2006

Executive Editor	Vivien Antwi
Executive Art Editor	Christine Keilty
Senior Editor	Peter Taylor
Copy-editor	Naomi Waters
Designer	Colin Goody
Picture Researchers	Jenny Faithfull
Production	Faizah Malik
Indexer	Sue Farr

ISBN 1 84533 163 X
A CIP catalogue record for this book is available from the British Library.

General Editor Dr John Stevenson

Contributors

Byzantium and the Rise of the West	Dr Peter Heather
The Middle Ages	Dr Andrew Bell
The Dawn of Modern Europe	Professor Andrew Pettegree

Typeset in Adobe Garamond, Gill Sans, Frutiger, Univers
Printed in China

Contents

Introduction

How Europe got its name is unknown. Herodotus, the Greek historian, wrote of three continents – Europe, Asia and Africa. The division of the world into three landmasses was therefore very ancient, but Herodotus confessed that he did not know why they had been given these names. The Greeks themselves initially used "Europe" to mean central Greece, but soon it meant the whole of the Greek mainland and the entire landmass to the north.

The boundary between Europe and Asia was usually fixed at the River Don in Russia, but knowledge of lands north of Greece and west of Sicily was sketchy. Gradually, however, the Mediterranean seaboard of Europe was explored. Early seafarers, possibly going back to Neolithic times, but certainly followed by Greeks and Phoenicians, ventured beyond the Straits of Gibraltar to the Atlantic coast of Europe. The great Greek geographer and astronomer, Ptolemy, working in Alexandria in the second century AD, gave co-ordinates of latitude and longitude for many of Europe's geographical features, though no maps based on them were produced until the Renaissance. The oldest medieval map – from the early 7th century – shows the three-part division of the world bounded by a great ocean. The first map of Europe dates from the early 12th century. Drawn up by Lambert, a canon of St. Omer in France, it remains the earliest illustration of Europe as a separate geographical entity.

Defining Europe

Today, our geographical grasp of the continent of Europe is clearer. Conventionally Europe is defined as the western part of the Eurasian land mass that forms one of the world's major land surfaces. Its boundary to the south lies at the Mediterranean, including the islands of Sicily and Crete. To the West, its boundary lies at the Atlantic Ocean and, to the north, at the Arctic Ocean and the Barents Sea. Its eastern boundary, however, is geographically indistinct. There are no great changes in flora or fauna to mark a point where Europe ends and Asia begins. Conventionally, the Ural Mountains, the Ural River, and the Caspian Sea are taken to denote the boundary between Europe and Asia. The great forests and marshes of the east have always lent a sense of remoteness to what we now know as Russia, but the world beyond the Urals, the vast trackless wastes of Siberia, became a by-word for remoteness and the very edge of European civilization. By convention,

too, Turkey lies in Asia, with Europe ending at the Bosporus, its frontier city the great metropolis of Istanbul, the former Constantinople.

The total land mass of Europe is about the same as the mainland USA, and was essentially defined by rising sea levels at the end of the last Ice Age, some 10,000 years ago, which separated the British Isles from the continent and defined the largely enclosed seas of the Baltic and the Mediterranean. The rise in sea levels gave Europe a coastline more extensive than any other continent in proportion to its size. Most of western Europe is relatively close to the sea, and even in the east great river systems assist in opening up the continent to maritime influences. Accordingly, it has been said that Europe was built for seafarers, and maritime trade has been undertaken from the earliest times. But Europe was also made for farmers and craftsmen. With much of the continent lying within the temperate zone and favoured by the Gulf Stream, it possesses extensive agricultural land, abundant timber and the essential fuels and raw materials for metalworking.

Irrespective of its geographical definition, Europe has a diverse political and cultural history, expressing different traditions going back to the earliest prehistoric civilizations. The political map of Europe we know today reflects the nation-states that have emerged over the past four or five centuries, and which were only taking shape when this volume of Europe's history is coming to an end. These states represent the emergence of consolidated centres of power out of the turmoil of the breakdown of the western Roman Empire and the invasion of new peoples and creeds from the eastern borderlands of Europe. It was a long process of transition, occupying the better part of 1000 years. Moreover, these processes do not always fit neatly into the definition of Europe set by geographers today. Russia, eventually extending right across the Eurasian landmass from the Baltic in the West to the Pacific in the East, has always straddled Europe and Asia. The south eastern boundaries of Europe, too, have always reflected ethnic and religious complexity, while contributing much to Europe's history. The power of the Ottoman Turks carried them west across the Bosporus into the Balkans where their empire lasted until the 19th century. The Mediterranean – the cradle of ancient civilization – has been both a boundary and a highway at different point in Europe's past. The Roman Empire straddled both Europe and Africa. Islamic states once existed on both sides of the Straits of Gibraltar in Muslim Spain and North Africa. Only in the period covered by this volume did the boundary between Christendom and Islam become divided by the Mediterranean.

People make their own borders, and rivalries in politics, religion, nationality and culture have imposed barriers almost irrespective of geography. Historically, Europe has been open to conquest and migration, absorbing new cultures and ideas. Before the age of mechanized transport, migration meant movements by foot, on horseback, by wagon, or by sail. This imposed a certain order and pace upon the changes that occurred, allowing different cultures to meld and to create new modified versions of what had existed before. Europe has been defined by its general cultural characteristics, by what became known as a distinctively "European civilization". This was seen as deriving from the ancient world, medieval Christendom, the Renaissance, and later the Enlightenment. This amalgam of ideas came to be widely understood as "European culture" and was transmitted at the time of European colonization to the rest of the world.

From Antiquity to the Renaissance

This series of books attempts to weave together these diverse threads into a coherent whole. In the previous volume, it discusses the beginnings of European history in the civilisations of the Aegean, the early Greeks who drew upon the culture of the Middle East, Egypt, and Crete to create what we know of as the Homeric age, celebrated through the great poet and his epic works after whom it is named. The details of that world are still being revealed by archaeologists, and the times of Homer and even earlier peoples still remain tantalizingly obscure. But the evolution of the Greek city-states represented a more tangible and accessible flowering of one of the greatest periods of human achievement. From them would emerge philosophical, cultural, and intellectual advances that would leave an enduring legacy for European and world civilization, shaping Europe's contribution to world culture and the way Europeans thought about themselves for centuries to come.

Even as the Greek city-states went into decline, Aristotle's pupil, Alexander, from the hitherto obscure kingdom of Macedon, blazed across the history of the Greek world and the Near East to create, in a few short years, the largest empire ever seen, reaching from the Balkans to India. With Alexander's death and the disintegration of his empire, a new and more durable power emerged. The rise of the Roman Republic and its domination of the Mediterranean world provided the basis for the creation of an empire that would eventually stretch from Scotland in the north to the Sahara in the south, and from the Atlantic in the west to the Euphrates in the east.

But the reach of Rome was not merely geographical; it left a permanent imprint on European civilization in its law, institutions and culture. The "barbarian" kingdoms that were to succeed the Roman Empire in the west were profoundly influenced by the world they conquered. The mutation of the eastern half of the Roman Empire, based in

E-1

An Anglo-Saxon map of the world, based probably on a Roman original, demonstrates a typically European-orientated view of the world, with the East at the top and the North to the left. The world surrounds an elongated Mediterranean Sea reaching from the bottom at the "Pillars of Hercules" – the modern Straits of Gibraltar – to Greece and Egypt.

F-1

Crusaders led by the French King Guy clash with the Ottoman forces, led by Saladin, in the seige of Acre, 1189–91. The first crusade was launched in 1095; the last took place nearly two centuries later.

Constantinople, into the Byzantine Empire carried Rome's legacy up to the very end of the Middle Ages. Not least of these legacies was Christianity. What had begun as a small persecuted sect from the distant Roman province of Judea, later known as Palestine, had become the official religion of the later Empire. Amidst the onslaught of barbarian, Slav, and Arab invasions, one of Rome's most profound legacies was the birth of medieval Christendom.

The world of Late Antiquity was under enormous pressures, subject to successive invasion and colonization. A millennium later, the situation was reversed: Europeans were undertaking the first great age of exploration — the voyages of Columbus and the Portuguese and Spanish explorers would found the first European empires. The foundations were laid for several centuries of European Christianity, until the Arab invasions brought Islam from Arabia, through North Africa and into the Iberian peninsula in the west.

Over the centuries, there would be an ebb and flow between Christian and Muslim power. Spain would be won and lost to Islam, eventually becoming the pillar of Christian and Catholic orthodoxy, forged in the fires of the *reconquista* ("reconquest"). The Christian West went on the offensive in the extraordinary series of invasions of the Near East known as the Crusades. A new Muslim power, the Ottoman Turks would carry their military successes by land to the heart of central Europe and the gates of Vienna. In the Mediterranean, the islands of Rhodes, Sicily, and Malta would become vital strategic points in the struggle between Christian and Muslim power at sea.

Europe's post-Roman history was one of growing subdivision and the consolidation of new forces. The tribes of central and northern Europe, the Slavs, the Arabs and the Vikings would recast Europe along new lines. Emerging from the new world order of late antiquity were a succession of powerful forces.

The barbarian kingdoms were consolidating in the West, eventually converting to Christianity, such as the Anglo-Saxon kingdoms in Britain and the Merovingians in Gaul. Amongst the most powerful to emerge was the Carolingian empire, carved out of the old Roman empire of the west. At its greatest extent c.800, it included Gaul, parts of Germany and much of Italy. These new states would eventually recognize the religious supremacy of the popes of Rome. To the east, the Byzantine Empire would foster a rival religious allegiance in the Orthodox Church, using the Greek language, eventually separating itself from the Latin Christendom of the West. It was Orthodox Christianity that was adopted by the Slavs and the early Russian state.

The Crusaders of the Latin West, initially cut right across the world of the Orthodox Greeks and the Byzantines, and attempted to establish permanent Latin Christian Kingdoms in the Holy Land. These attempts ultimately failed, and the borders of Christian Europe were put once more onto the defensive by the rise of the formidable power of the Ottoman Turks. Indeed, against the onslaught of the Ottoman armies and fleets, it appeared that the boundaries of Christian Europe would be forced to give way, as the Turks conquered Constantinople in 1453, sweeping into the Balkans and threatening central Europe.

For more than two centuries, the boundaries of Christian Europe rested upon the military balance between the Christian powers and the Turks. The Ottoman threat was only blunted with their defeat at Lepanto in 1571 and their last siege of Vienna in 1683. Hungary, long in dispute between the Christian Habsburgs and the Ottomans, finally fell back into Christian control. Elsewhere in Europe, Latin Christianity had overcome its enemies, defeating the Muslim kingdoms of Spain and eventually forcing the conversion or expulsion of the remaining Muslim inhabitants. In the north the Teutonic Knights waged war on pagan or Orthodox Slavs in the name of a new Crusade. Crusading impetus was also turned inwards against heretical groups such as the Cathars. With the power of Byzantium now destroyed by Ottoman conquest, Orthodox Russia would remain in conflict with the Turks for another century, its frontiers still contested into the modern era.

Even as the Christian powers grappled with the Ottoman threat, the unity of Christendom was being fractured. Orthodoxy remained unreconciled to Rome, and in the 16th century the Protestant Reformation shattered the unity of medieval Christendom still further. Protestantism and the Counter-Reformation were to plunge Europe into wars of religion and decades of religious controversy.

Emerging nation-states were now often to define themselves through their religion. As in Protestant England or Lutheran Sweden, religious persuasion gave an impulse to forging stronger states, forcing them into self-conscious rivalry with powers such as Catholic Spain or Habsburg Europe. Europe emerged from the wars of religion with stronger nation-states, now organized for international conflict and, in many cases, under absolutist rulers.

Exploration and Renaissance

A fresh dimension was added to European history as Europe asserted itself overseas. Less than 40 years after the fall of Constantinople, Columbus made his first landfall in Hispaniola in the Caribbean, opening up the New World to European conquest and colonization. The age of exploration created the first European empires in South and Central America, with the Spanish conquests of the Aztec and Inca empires. This brought untold wealth from the New World to Europe, although at a terrible price to native conquered peoples. European influence was soon being felt in Africa, the Indian Ocean, and the Far East. Portuguese navigators opened up the sea routes into the South Atlantic and around Africa, undertaking the first circumnavigation. Soon they were followed by Dutch, British, and French traders and missionaries. By 1600, Jesuit missionaries were at work as far afield as California, Peru, India, and Japan. The first colonies had by that time been planted in North America, and British and French traders were plundering the cod fisheries off Newfoundland and the rich fur trade of the North America interior. Europe was on the verge of establishing a worldwide network of trade and dominion, which would find its apogee after 1700.

Europe's intellectual horizons were also expanding. Christianity had provided for the transmission of large amounts of ancient knowledge and scholarship to medieval Europe, through the efforts of intellectual giants such as Thomas Aquinas. But much had been lost, and it was often through Arab texts that much of the learning of antiquity in areas such as medicine, astronomy and mathematics was passed on. The fall of Byzantium brought a fresh wave of learning from the Greek world into Europe, greatly stimulating the intellectual ferment of the West as the Ottoman world stagnated. European thought, stimulated anew by the models of the ancient world and the challenges of exploration was to reach new heights of artistic, intellectual and scientific progress by the early modern period. From the Renaissance and the Scientific Revolution, Europe would leap forward again in the centuries to come to produce startling progress in ideas and material progress.

THE RISE OF THE WEST

700–1000

POLITICS AND GOVERNMENT

F-2

771 Charlemagne is crowned sole king of the Franks. He conquers Lombardy and is crowned King of the Lombards in 774. In 772, he embarks on the conquest of Saxony, which was completed in 802.

793 The sack of the island monastery of Lindisfarne marks the opening of fierce Viking raiding upon Western Europe.

751 Creation of the Papal States.

714–41 Reign of Charles Martel reunifies Francia after the collapse of Merovingian unity in the 7th century.

F-3

700   775

SOCIETY AND CULTURE

*c.*732–87 First Iconoclasm in Byzantium.

*c.*750 onwards introduction of manorialized agriculture in Western Europe increases total output, but cements social divides between landlords and peasants.

789 The *Admonitio Generalis* marks Charlemagne's efforts to reform Christian observance in the areas under his rule.

F-4

*c.*700 production of the *Codex Amiatinus* in Northumbria, with fabulous illuminations in a realistic, classicizing style.

F-2

679–754 St Boniface, the "Apostle of Germany", missionary and Church reformer who spreads the Gospel in Germany and the Low countries until his martyrdom.

G-1

814–43 Second Iconoclasm in Byzantium.

*c.*830 Classicizing illustrations of the Utrecht Psalter.

*c.*740–804 Alcuin of York: leading Christian scholar of his day and one of the architects of the revival of learning under Charlemage – the Carolingian Renaissance.

*c.*820–50 Great era of Carolingian Church construction: huge basilicas with apses and towers at each end such as St. Riquier and as advocated in the paradigmatic Plan of St Gall.

1066 William of Normandy conquers England to create new cross-channel superstate in Western Europe.

911 Licensed settlement of the Vikings of Rollo around Rouen on the Seine: the first act in the creation of the Duchy of Normandy.

888 Deposition of Charles the Fat marks the end of the Carolingian imperial period in the West.

Ȝ-2

962 Imperial coronation of Otto I in Rome marks the creation of the Holy Roman Empire based on the Duchy of Saxony.

865–78 The first Viking great army in England conquers Northumbria, Mercia, and East Anglia.

E-3

983 Revolt of the Elbe Slavs against Saxon domination.

925

1000

*c.*860 Cyril and Methodius create the first written version of Slavic to translate the Bible.

*c.*920–89 Christianization of new states of Slavic Europe: Bohemia, Poland, and Kievan Russia.

1054 The Great Schism marks a culmination of papal self-assertion.

909/10 Foundation of the monastery of Cluny in Burgundy opens new era of monastic federations operating independent of lay patrons and answering to the Pope.

On Christmas Day 800,
Charlemagne was crowned
emperor in St Peters in Rome,
reviving the concept of empire in
Western Europe. This bronze
equestrian statue in miniature,
produced in about 870, celebrates
his glory. It portrays him with the
orb that symbolized, after Roman
models, his world domination.

NEW EMPIRES

In the period c.700–1000, new imperial powers emerged in a post-Roman West freed from Mediterranean domination. The greatest of these empires was that of the Frankish Carolingian dynasty. In the 8th century, it united all of Francia west of the Rhine, then added Germany up to the Elbe, most of Italy, and a large part of central Europe. The title of emperor was revived on Christmas Day 800 to crown the achievements of the dynasty's greatest member: Charles the Great – Charlemagne.

Carolingian domination was built on the exploitation of extraordinary sources of wealth, rather than on developed governmental institutions. When the wealth ran out, as it did in the 9th century, the basic situation that had evolved in the post-Roman West still applied: power tended to move from the centre to localities. In the 9th and 10th centuries, this was reinforced by two longer term developments. First, in the manorialized estates, landlords evolved a more intensive form of agricultural exploitation that allowed them to generate a much greater income from the same area of landed holding. As kings had no general rights to tax their landowners, the latter grew in power and wealth compared to their kings. At the same time, defensive armour and castle-building was making military activity an elite profession and distancing landlords from lesser mortals. A dominant, militarized, landowning oligarchy thus came to power in the localities. Where kings lost access to external sources of wealth, as in West Francia (now France) from the later 9th century, this oligarchy came to establish its almost complete independence of monarchical centres.

In East Francia (now Germany), the Carolingian line ran out earlier, but centralized government survived. In the first half of the 10th century, through Henry I and his son Otto I, the ducal line of Saxony advanced first to royal, then imperial status. This success was based partly, like the Carolingians, on having extraordinary sources of wealth to fund the acquisition of supporters, but also on providing effective leadership against the nomadic Magyars who had moved into the Hungarian Plain in the 890s. Otto led the east Franks to final victory over the Magyars in 955, then brought both Italy and the newly emerging Slavic monarchies of central Europe into his political orbit.

Scandinavian populations also came to play a major role in European history during this period. By 800, they had developed the naval technology to form closer ties with the rest of Europe. Some traded, while others – the Vikings – raided and eventually, from c.850, formed larger armies in order to conquer areas for settlement. Further east in northern Russia, Scandinavian traders extracted furs and slaves, and quickly discovered the river routes that allowed them to sell their goods in the rich markets of the Islamic Near East. As a whole, the Viking period generated a wide range of consequences. Many new trading relationships were established across Europe, new settlements were established in England and northern France, and new states – both in Scandinavia itself and in Russia – came into existence.

From one of the settlements, that around Rouen, Normandy was to emerge: the last of the new western empires. In the 10th century, the Scandinavian rulers of Rouen united other Viking groups behind them and played the political game in the wider arena of West Francia. By 1000, they had proclaimed themselves dukes of Normandy, and, in 1066, in the person of William the Conqueror, stepped up to become kings of a state that spanned the Channel. Lesser Normans were also highly active, moving vigorously into Celtic Britain and, above all, southern Italy, to create a wider Norman empire.

Charlemagne's Empire

On Christmas Day 800, Charlemagne entered St Peters in Rome as King of the Franks and left it as Emperor of the West. He would later say that had he known what Pope Leo III was about to do, he would have stayed outside. This was an obligatory show of modesty. Charlemagne and his advisers had been working towards the imperial title for a decade.

Charlemagne's silver coinage set a standard for all of Western Europe and is a sign of increasing monetary exchange. This silver penny, minted at the trading port of Quentovic (near modern Boulogne), was also used to celebrate his new imperial status, styling him imperator (imp) *and* augustus (aug)*, the characteristic titles of Roman emperors.*

F - 6

Charlemagne's palace complex at Aachen in North Rhine-Westphalia was modelled on the great palace in Constantinople, but with important modifications. Both had thrones in their main Churches, but where Byzantine emperors sat in the east behind the high altar, Charlemage deliberately placed himself more modestly in the west, criticizing their claims to rule "with God" as hubris.

F - 7

The rise of the Pepinids

By 700, the kingdom of the Merovingian Franks had fragmented. Charlemagne's ancestors first rose to prominence as the dominant aristocratic dynasty in one of its now largely autonomous regions: north-eastern France and Belgium (known as Austrasia). The new dynasty's rise to more general dominance was secured by Charlemagne's grandfather Charles Martel. Securely in control of Austrasia from 714, he defeated in 719 a coalition of rivals from the other regions of Francia: north-western France (known as Neustria), Aquitaine, and Burgundy. By the time of his famous victory over the Muslim Arabs at Poitiers in 732, he had reunited Francia and begun to restore its hegemony east of the Rhine. After the death of his Merovingian figurehead, Theoderic IV, in 737, Charles also operated for his last years as an entirely independent ruler, although he stepped back from claiming the royal title. Charles was succeeded in 741

by his two sons Pepin and Carloman, but a major aristocratic revolt convinced them to find another Merovingian frontman. They duly promoted Childeric III, but after Carloman retired to a monastery and his own power was secure, Pepin finally procured sufficient support to take the royal title. Childeric was deposed, and Pepin promoted to kingship in 751. One of a peer group of regional aristocrats had succeeded in elbowing himself into power above his rivals.

Charlemagne and the Carolingian Empire

The dynasty was to reach new heights in the next generation. In a series of dramatic conquests, Pepin's son Charlemagne – "Charles the Great" – extended his rule over most of central and Western Europe. South of the Pyrenees, Charlemagne's reach never went much beyond Barcelona, but elsewhere his successes were astonishing. East of the Rhine, Alamannia, Thuringia, and Bavaria were quickly taken over. Further north, Saxony, too, was eventually conquered in 804, but only after 30 years of fierce resistance. South of the Alps, the entire Lombard kingdom was conquered in 774, and, in central Europe, the 200-year-old Avar Empire was dismantled in the 790s. By the year 800, Charlemagne's fiat extended from the Atlantic to the Elbe, and from the Baltic to Rome.

Not surprisingly, the king and his advisers searched for a suitable means of expressing Charlemagne's new grandeur; they also contemplated the significance of his unprecedented success. As devout Christians who believed that God directly intervened in world affairs, they could only conclude that He was behind the victories and that God's aim was to restore the concept of empire in the West, which had been lost with the collapse of Rome. "Empire" not only indicated a scale of rule that was beyond that of a mere king, but also in the Roman imperial ideology still strongly preserved in Constantinople, carried connotations of a special relationship with God. Charlemagne and his advisers were reaching out towards the imperial title from 790 at the latest. From that point, they began to criticize parts of the Byzantines' vision of empire, accusing them of arrogance in claiming that their emperor ruled "with God". Charlemagne also set about a general reform of Christian observance. Charlemagne's decrees stated that this was the service he owed God in return for victory. Contemporary popes were hesitant about the implicit challenge to their own religious pre-eminence; however, Leo III was eventually put in the position of needing Charlemagne's support against rivals in Rome who were seeking to depose and blind him. Charlemagne came to the city in the winter of 800. He convened a special council on 24 December 800, which confirmed Leo in office, and was himself crowned emperor on Christmas Day.

Empire in action

The imperial title marked not so much the beginning of a new stage in Charlemagne's reign, as a recognition of all that he had already achieved. Afterwards, his religious aims were strongly restated, and the running of the Empire continued much as before. What stands out are the fundamental differences between the Frankish version of empire and how the Roman model had operated four centuries before. The Frankish Empire operated without a designated political capital (or capitals), and with no extensive administrative bureaucracy. The loyalty of local landowning elites was secured by a non-stop process of travel and supervision, rather than by offering them jobs in a huge governmental machine. Charlemagne, except when old age confined him to his spa palace at Aachen, was an itinerant monarch who averaged 30km (8 miles) a day throughout his reign. This allowed local men and king reciprocal access, the king checking on their loyalty and offering them in return the chance to ask him for personal favours. A key element was the annual assembly of militarized landowners on the eve of the year's campaigning season, where they and the king could deal with pressing business. The decisions of such councils sometimes acquired written form (known as capitularies), but these were aides-mémoires reflecting an essentially oral process, rather than formal written decrees after the Roman pattern.

The king had no professional army of any size separate from these landowners and their followers, and his wealth came from landholding, not developed taxation rights. In geographical scale, the Carolingian Empire matched that of the old Roman West, but in methods of government it was simply a larger version of the kind of state that had replaced the Roman Empire after its collapse, rather than an entity of an entirely different kind.

F. 8

Charlemagne's reign saw major new conquests, turning most of Western Europe into one imperial state. This empire was not governed through an administrative bureaucracy, however. Averaging 30 kilometres (8 miles) a day, Charlemagne himself travelled between a network of palaces and other stopping points to gather information, collect revenues and cow potential rebels.

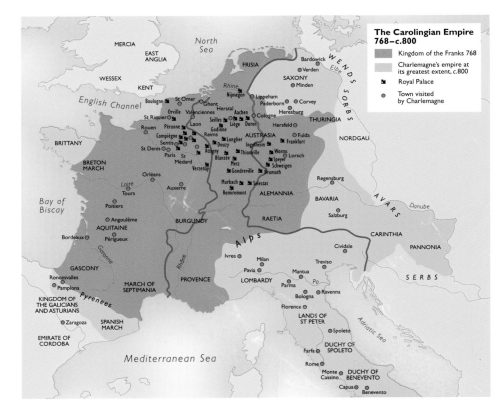

The Carolingian Empire
768–c.800

■ Kingdom of the Franks 768
▢ Charlemagne's empire at its greatest extent, c.800
🏰 Royal Palace
● Town visited by Charlemagne

Feudalism and Carolingian Decline

The Carolingian Empire was based on personal relationships among the landowning elites of Western Europe, rather than bureaucratic government. A key element was the feudal bond between unequal partners: lord and vassal. The relationship was built on defined services on the part of the vassal – military and other – in return for tenure of a piece of the lord's land and his judicial protection.

The growth of local power

These relationships were built against the backdrop of two much longer term trends that favoured the growth of local power. First, the basis of agricultural production was slowly transformed between the 7th and 11th centuries. The landed properties of the wealthy – starting with monasteries, but spreading to secular lords – were revolutionized by the growth of manorial agriculture, which placed new wealth in the hands of the lords and depressed the status of many previously free peasants. At the same time, advances in the fields of defensive armour and castle-building changed patterns of warfare – and social relations – out of all recognition. While armour rendered large but ill-equipped armies redundant, it was very expensive. Hence warfare became largely confined

F-9

Under Charlemagne's grandsons, the Empire seemed undiminished. Government was increasingly bureaucratic and court culture flourished, especially under Charles the Bald, pictured here enthroned in majesty between personifications of his main territories, Franconia and Gothia. Beneath the imperial veneer, however, socio-economic change was cementing in place the dominance of more local landowners.

to the manor-holding class and their immediate retainers. Fortifications allowed small numbers of men to tie up large numbers of opponents, so that castles were built both by kings and regional lords in large numbers after *c*.850. This, too, had important social effects. Even a small-scale local lord, if in charge of a castle, could dominate his locality and be very difficult to oust.

Feudalism and Carolingian collapse

Charlemagne had initially planned to divide the Empire between three sons, but the eldest was to be given a dominant share together with the imperial title. By the time of Charlemagne's death in 814, only Louis the Pious survived, so he inherited everything. Louis was survived by four adult sons, who expected and extracted equal shares of land. They had even tried to take shares of power from their father in the 830s. On Louis' death in 843, the Empire was evenly divided, and his sons quickly fell out among themselves. Two in particular – Charles the Bald in the west and Louis the German in the east – survived the initial rounds of competition and rivalry. By the 850s, they were campaigning against one another and had recruited dedicated bodies of supporters for the same purpose.

At the same time, Viking raids were growing in intensity, particularly in the realm of Charles the Bald, and centralized direction was far too cumbersome to fight off these raiders' unpredictable assaults. It became necessary, therefore, for the two kings both to reward their supporters in the battle for primacy and to cede local control to subordinates to run the defensive war against the Vikings.

These processes had dramatic results. The Carolingians were dependent upon military expansion to compensate for a deficiency in internally derived revenues. Aggressive warfare had continued steadily from Charles Martel to Charlemagne, but came to an end in the reign of Louis the Pious. From that point onwards, rewards for political supporters had to be made largely out of the capital stock of royal lands – itself divided between Louis' various sons – with consequences for royal power that exactly mirrored the fate of the Merovingians. The delegation of power in the western kingdom to fight the Vikings only hurried the process along. By the end of Charles the Bald's reign in 877, direct royal landholding in the west was limited only to northern areas around Paris. Elsewhere, control had passed into the hands of numerous regional and still more local lords. When Charles' immediate successor, Charles the Fat, proved an incapable war-leader against the Vikings, he was deposed and, as the contemporary Regino of Prüm put it, "each area made its own king out of its bowels".

Medieval manorial agriculture

Carolingian lords increasingly ran their estates as centrally directed productive units – ie, manors. A legally tied peasantry provided for its own needs from independent tenements in return for substantial amounts of labour that was used to farm a separate portion of the estate – the demesne. The new regime allowed landlords to introduce more productive three-crop rotations and make economies of scale in such expensive items as plough teams. As a result, the agricultural year became a regular succession of monthly tasks that were often illustrated in calendar form. This Anglo-Saxon manuscript of *c*.1050 portrays the reaping and gathering of the August harvest.

New patterns of power

These political events intersected with the underlying trends in favour of the growth of local power to generate a variety of outcomes. East of the Rhine, in the kingdom of Louis the German, the 10th century saw considerable unity maintained for very particular reasons under the new Ottonian dynasty. In western Francia and Italy, there was greater variety. Particularly in the north, the later Carolingians (restored in the person of Louis IV d'Outremer ["from over the sea"] in 936–54), some of their trusted lieutenants in the Viking war (especially the Robertians from whom the later Capetian royal dynasty evolved), and several other dynasts, such as the Dukes of Flanders, kept control of substantial regional power blocks. They had learnt from the earlier Carolingian example and quickly adopted primogeniture – succession of the first-born son – to prevent any further erosions of central power. These rulers were thus able to enjoy the fruits of manorialization themselves and keep castle-building firmly under their own control.

Elsewhere, however, power quickly devolved into the hands of local castle-holders – castellans – who became a fixed, hereditary feature of the landscape. In their own localities, the castellans quickly abrogated to themselves previously royal rights over markets, coinage, taxation, and labour dues to establish a domination which would last throughout the medieval period.

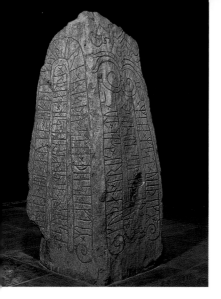

The Vikings

In the 9th and 10th centuries, Scandinavian adventurers took to Europe's seas and rivers to make money in every possible way. From the North Sea to the Caspian, the Vikings sold furs and slaves, conducted raids, and extracted tributes. Where circumstances were right, they even settled and became new elites. The overall result of these actions was an enormous flow of wealth into Scandinavia which generated social and political revolution.

The Viking age brought momentous change to the Scandinavian homelands. By 1000 a new aristocracy, its dominance erected on the back of wealth from overseas, was declaring its recently won control of landed resources by erecting title deeds in the form of carved rune stones, such as this one from Jutland in Denmark.

From *c.*800, Viking raids upon Western Europe became commonplace. The raiders targeted wealthy monasteries in addition to the now well-established trading centres of the Channel. The important port of Dorestad at the mouth of the Rhine was attacked four times in the 830s alone. Around 850, the attacks grew in intensity: a process marked by Viking attackers overwintering in the West rather than going home, and by the appearance in contemporary sources of named Viking leaders. It culminated in the era of "great armies", which started in England in 865.

Previously separate raiding groups were now amalgamated into composite armies, numbering between 5000 and 10,000 men. Their increased power allowed them to conquer entire kingdoms and was probably the reason that they had banded together in the first place. Between 865 and 874, the first great army led by a coalition of kings, including the brothers Ingvar and Halfdan, conquered Northumbria, half of Mercia (roughly the region that is now the Midlands), and East Anglia. Its ravages were finally checked by Alfred the Great of Wessex at Eddington in 878. The victory prevented further conquests, but did not reverse the land seizures taking place in territories already conquered. Checked in England, the Vikings who had not won land there turned to northern France and the Low Countries, where they ravaged widely from 879–92. A further assault – again frustrated by Alfred – was made on southern England from 892–5, before the remaining unsatisfied Vikings made their return to the continent once more.

The main outcomes of this activity were two-fold: large-scale transfers of western wealth to Scandinavia and the establishment of a series of Scandinavian enclaves in the West. Danelaw, comprising most of eastern England, was the largest of these, but, on the continent, there were settlements at the mouths of

By c.800, major advances in Scandinavian ship construction had made the world a much smaller place. Merchant adventurers ranged across the Atlantic and down the river routes of Eastern Europe. Close on their heels came raiders and settlers. The result was revolution by integration. New Scandinavian-dominated entities were generated outside of the Baltic region from Greenland to northern Russia, and wealth poured into Scandinavia itself, generating a struggle for power from which there emerged new state structures in Denmark, Norway, and Sweden.

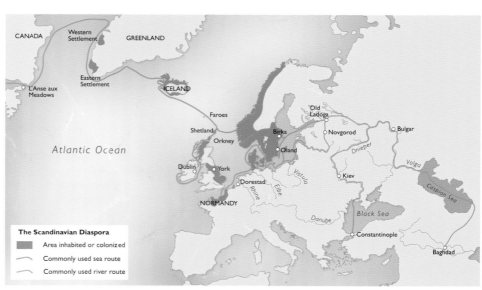

The Scandinavian Diaspora

▢ Area inhabited or colonized

── Commonly used sea route

── Commonly used river route

the Seine in Normandy and the Loire, and a number of coastal communities established themselves in Ireland. Northern Scotland, Shetland, Orkney, and the western isles as far south as Man were also overrun.

Vikings of Russia

At the same time, other Scandinavians, known to the indigenous Finns as "Rus", had been making money further east, trading slaves, furs, and other products from the subarctic forest world of northern Russia. Their first permanent colony there, around Lake Ladoga, was established in *c.*750. At this stage, the extracted goods were being traded back through the Baltic to the West. Very quickly, however, the Norsemen realized that the river routes of western Russia provided access to much richer markets. South-flowing river networks, particularly those around the Dnieper and Volga, led from the subarctic north to the Black and Caspian Seas and on to the rich world of medieval Islam, where the Abbasid Caliphate was at its height. By *c.*800, the first flows of Muslim silver coin – given in return for furs and slaves – were reaching the Baltic, but it was from about 880 onwards that the stream became a flood.

By this stage, the Viking merchants were no longer making the long trek south to the Caspian, but were trading with Islamic merchants in the markets of the Volga Bulgars. By *c.*900, several distinct Scandinavian settlements had established themselves in northern Russia, all under the control of the Rurikid dynasty (named after Ruric, their founder), the seat of which was established on the island fortress of Gorodische. These princes also quickly brought under their control a second set of settlements further south on the middle Dnieper, particularly at Kiev, which had begun a substantial, if secondary, trade with Constantinople.

In the later 10th and 11th centuries, as Islamic collapse rendered trade less profitable, the Rurikids developed more regular patterns of revenue generation, based on the productive capacities of surrounding Slavic tribes, and itinerant governmental structures to control them. From the extended Viking trading company of the early 9th century developed the first, Kievan, Russian state.

Viking-age Scandinavia

The Viking age also transformed Scandinavia. In the 8th century, southern Denmark was dominated by powerful chieftains capable of organizing major public works, such as the Danewirke, a defensive ditch and wooden wall along the southern edge of the Jutland peninsula. These political structures were far from stable and were exercised over a restricted geographical area. The flow of wealth from east and west in the Viking age completely undermined them.

The Gokstad Ship
Excavated in the late 19th century, the beautiful 9th-century Gokstad ship, now in the Oslo Museum, provides one of the keys to the Viking age. Up to the 7th century, Scandinavian boats were oar-propelled canoes, designed for river work and the island archipelagos of the Baltic. The Gokstad ship illustrates the changes that occurred over the next century. Clinker-built spars attached to a one-piece central keel created a hull of great strength, and sails were added to drive the ships over vast distances. The advances came from the Viking's desire to participate in new trading networks that grew up in the North and Baltic Seas between 650 and 800.

The dominance of the old rulers was based on the control of purely Scandinavian resources, and they could not compete with those who returned home with overseas wealth. By 850, the old structures had collapsed and power fragmented. Larger political structures were finally re-established only from the mid-10th century when, with overseas wealth subsiding, the Jelling dynasty of Gorm and his son Harold Bluetooth united the Jutland peninsula and its adjacent islands (Sjaelland, Skåne, and Fyn). Over the next century, their successors were able to create a genuine state.

After *c.*980, no more Muslim silver flowed into the Baltic, and Svein and Canute (son and grandson of Harold) put themselves at the head of further expansionary activity in the West. Between *c.*995 and 1016, they conquered the whole of England, thus creating a true Viking empire. The empire did not outlive Canute, its founder, but the period was used to develop stable political institutions at home: the kingdom of Denmark had been born. The two centuries after the turn of the millennium saw the evolution of similarly solid structures in neighbouring Norway and Sweden.

The Ottonians

When the line of Louis the German – Charlemagne's grandson – ran out, the dukes of Saxony, Bavaria, Alamannia, Swabia, and Lotharingia competed for overall power. From the 920s, the Ottonian dukes of Saxony emerged to make themselves undisputed kings of East Francia and even to revive the Carolingian tradition of empire.

The rise of the Liudolfings

Liudolf (*d.* 866) began his career as a Carolingian appointee: commander on the Elbe frontier in his native Saxony. His grandson Henry I (the Fowler: Duke of Saxony from 912 and King of East Francia from 919–36) was able to take his family's pre-eminence a stage further, primarily because of the military leadership which he provided against the Magyars. The Magyars were a nomadic grouping who had moved into the grasslands of the Hungarian Plain in the 890s. From there, they mounted a series of raids across Europe and larger campaigns into the neighbouring East Frankish kingdom, where they inflicted a series of heavy defeats on its ducal-led armies in the 900s and 910s. Henry negotiated a truce with the Magyars in 926 and used the respite to undertake military reforms. Garrisoned forts were constructed throughout the kingdom, and he turned the Saxon field army into heavy armoured cavalry. When war resumed, the forts made it impossible for the Magyars to extract easy booty, and the new Saxon army was able to inflict a first defeat upon the nomads at the battle of Riade in 933. This leadership propelled Henry to kingship over all of East Francia, although his prominence was disputed, especially by the Bavarian ducal line. Throughout his reign, Henry operated as *primus inter pares* ("first among equals"), with an ideology of *amicitia* ("friendship") towards the other dukes.

Empire

The dynasty acquired imperial status under Henry's son Otto I (936–73). Early in his reign, Otto faced challenges from members of his own family, who often combined against him with other East Frankish Dukes. Otto overcame these revolts and even used them to cement his position, replacing the indigenous ducal line of Bavaria with his younger brother Henry in 947. His ability to do this was based on two extraordinary resources unique to Saxony, which had also sustained his father. First, the silver mines of the Harz Mountains provided the Saxon ducal line with great wealth. At the same time, colonial expansion beyond the Elbe into Slavic territories gave it large amounts of new land with which to reward followers in the marches. Exploitation of these areas reached a new peak under Otto, who also undertook the Christianization of the conquered Slavs, establishing a series of missionary bishoprics under the rule of a new Archbishopric at Magdeburg. With a ready supply of new rewards, he could secure the loyalty of old magnates and attract new supporters. His consequent military strength allowed him to defeat internal challenges and administer a final coup de grâce to Magyar expansionism in 955 at the battle of the Lech. Thereafter, the Magyars quickly converted to Christianity and joined the club of Western Christendom. Otto's successes also opened up the path to Italy, where he again conquered much new territory and intervened in the Papal State. Otto steadily replaced local Italians with churchmen from northern Europe interested in continuing the Carolingian projects of reform. The policy bore fruit in 962 when Otto was crowned emperor in Rome by Pope John XII.

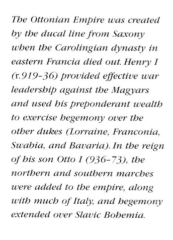

The Ottonian Empire was created by the ducal line from Saxony when the Carolingian dynasty in eastern Francia died out. Henry I (r.919-36) provided effective war leadership against the Magyars and used his preponderant wealth to exercise hegemony over the other dukes (Lorraine, Franconia, Swabia, and Bavaria). In the reign of his son Otto I (936-73), the northern and southern marches were added to the empire, along with much of Italy, and hegemony extended over Slavic Bohemia.

The Ottonian Empire 936–72

Ottonian Empire 936
Additions to Ottonian Empire by 972

Like the Carolingians before them, the Ottonians used classicizing pictorial models to express their imperial power. Here, from his magnificently illustrated Coronation Gospels, *the power of Otto II is represented by female personifications of dependent territories bringing him free offerings of their agricultural produce as tribute.*

The golden age

Otto's coronation heralded a new golden age. His son Otto II married a Byzantine princess, Theophanou, and their court was celebrated for its magnificent culture. Writing blossomed, splendid metalwork was created, and a series of beautiful illuminated manuscripts was produced. Into the orbit of this imperial greatness were drawn the new, largely Slavic monarchies of central and Eastern Europe: Poland, Bohemia, and Russia. Each of these states had been built around a core territory of dense settlement ringed with royal castles. From these core areas, the new monarchies dismantled old tribal structures in their immediate surroundings and squabbled with their peers. Their political history is marked, therefore, by great rises and falls, as the strong man from first one of the monarchies, then another, temporarily added vast tracts of Eastern Europe to his core powerbase. In cultural terms, Russia moved partly in a Byzantine orbit, but Poland, Bohemia, the new Magyar monarchy, and the territories in between became part of a larger Ottonian hegemony. The great symbolic moment came in AD 1000, when Otto III (king from 983; emperor 996–1002), grandson of Otto I, made an imperial progress to Poland, inaugurating the independent Christian province of Poland under its own archbishop at Gniezno.

The limits of the Ottonian Empire

Like its Carolingian predecessor, the Ottonian Empire had limitations. Within East Francia, powerful ducal structures remained, and imperial landholding and travel were largely limited to Saxony itself. The Ottonians' ability to dominate this constellation of dukes was based on its unique access to extraordinary sources of wealth, and, in the later 10th century, this was cut off. Muslim forces inflicted a huge defeat on the Emperor Otto II at Cap Colonne in 982. This setback, closely followed by Otto's relatively early death, provided the Elbe Slavs with the opportunity to throw off colonial domination. A huge, co-ordinated revolt throughout the marchlands in 983 reestablished Slavic independence and was marked by a rejection of Christianity. Otto III also failed to produce an heir, so that the imperial title passed at this point to the Salians, descendants of Otto I's younger brother Henry, whom he had installed in Bavaria. By this time, the power sources that had made Otto so dominant were ebbing away, and the Holy Roman Empire, the state he created, began its evolution from imperial power to electoral commonwealth.

The Normans

Normandy had its origins in a licensed settlement of Vikings on the Upper Seine in 911. By the end of the century, it had become a powerful, autonomous duchy. The new state preserved Viking expansionary traditions. Both its dukes and lesser nobility were ready to seize every available opportunity, so that, by 1100, Normans were running much of the British Isles and large parts of France and southern Italy.

From settlement to duchy

The career details of the first leader of the Rouen Vikings, Rollo, are lost in the mists of time. Defeated by the Franks at Chartres in 910, he was baptized and settled on the Upper Seine to guard the region against other Vikings. This was one of several such settlements at the time – with others occurring in Brittany and the Loire – and was probably part of the fall-out from the second great army repulsed from England in the mid-890s. The power of the Rouen settlement and its leaders grew in stages. In the 930s, William Longsword, Rollo's son, started to play a more prominent role in the political rivalries of the great magnates of north-western Francia: Carolingian kings, Capetian lords, and counts of Flanders. For his troubles, he was granted further lands west of Rouen, but paid for them with his life: in 942, Count Arnulf of Flanders, one of his main opponents, organized his assassination. Under William's son, Richard I (Count of Rouen 945–96), more land came under the dynasty's control, its remit now stretching west to Bayeux and the Cotentin and south to Evreux. Much of this success was based on the great wealth deriving from Rouen's position as one of the great trading centres of northern Europe, wealth which came to

the dynasty in taxes and tolls. From Richard I's time, the rulers of Normandy thus maintained a substantial coinage, and many coin hoards have been found, the largest a spectacular 8586 coins at Fecamp. The rise of Normandy within Francia reached its apogee under Richard II. Shortly before he entertained the Frankish king at Fecamp in 1006, he began to use the title *dux* (duke) and to appoint a series of counts to the territories within his domains. This grand title reflected the greater expanse of territory under his control and his ability to extract recognition from his contemporaries.

The conquest of England

The size and position of the new duchy gave it an important role in international affairs. In the early 11th century, the Vikings returned to England, and Ethelred ("the Unready") wanted to prevent the raiders from using Normandy as a base. Richard II's daughter Emma became his queen, and, when his dynasty was ousted from England by Canute in 1016, his surviving children sought refuge in Normandy. After 1042, when Canute's line gave out, Ethelred's grandson, Edward the Confessor, returned to England, but retained close connections with his adopted homeland. He occupied a very difficult political situation, facing over-mighty subjects in the family of the Earl of Wessex: Godwin and his son Harold. Having no children, Edward sought to protect his position by making an outsider his heir; he could not have chosen a Godwin, or they would have sidelined him completely. He naturally turned to Normandy and Richard II's bastard son William. He kept some independence, but, in the longer term, the result could only be war. The Godwins would never accept a Norman ruler, and the Normans could not tolerate them. When Edward died in 1066, therefore, Harold seized the throne and William invaded. In the great showdown just outside Hastings, Harold and his brothers were killed: the Norman ducal line had now become a royal one. William proceeded to

F - VI

The Domesday Book of 1086 contains an astonishingly detailed survey of the English towns and countryside. The annual income of each unit of production was valued in monetary terms, and many assets (labour force, ploughs, etc) were individually listed. The results, organized by landowner, provide a clear account of exactly who gained what from the Norman Conquest.

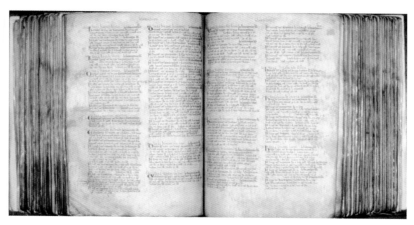

reward the supporters who had backed him so effectively. By 1086, as recorded in the Domesday Book, the landowning class of Anglo-Saxon England had been almost entirely replaced by Normans (for example, only six out of 180 chief landowners were Anglo-Saxons).

This new state, spanning the English Channel, was one of the richest in Europe, and, in the first generations, its rulers retained their Norman orientation. William the Conqueror and his sons divided their time two-thirds to one-third between Normandy and England, and essentially used the wealth of England to further their continental political ambitions, in particular to fend off the power of their notional overlords, the kings of France.

Wider horizons

From their continental and later English bases, individual Norman magnates quickly moved into Wales and Scotland in the 11th century, and Ireland in the 12th century. The most dramatic example of Norman magnate-led expansion occurred, however, in southern Italy. In the early 11th century the region was politically fragmented. The Lombard princes of Benevento, Salerno, and Capua were fighting among themselves and against Byzantine overlordship. The need for mercenaries was strong, and Norman warlords and their men found employment in ever-increasing numbers.

In 1030, the erstwhile employees began the process of turning themselves into masters. They seized the Calabrian town of Aversa; Melfi followed in 1041, then attacks were made on the Byzantines in Apulia and Calabria, who turned to the papacy for assistance. At the battle of Civitate in 1053, Pope Leo IX was captured by the Normans, and a great realignment followed. The papacy switched its backing to the Normans, formally granting their leaders lands they had not yet conquered in the Investiture of Melfi on 2 March 1059, lands which still belonged to the Byzantines and Muslims. Richard of Aversa was proclaimed the legitimate ruler of Capua; Robert Guiscard that of Calabria, Apulia, and Sicily. Guiscard quickly turned theory into practice, conquering Calabria in 1060 and Apulia in 1071.

Meanwhile, Guiscard's brother Roger turned his attention to Muslim-held Sicily. The invasion began in 1061, and made slow, steady progress. Palermo was captured in 1072, and final victory eventually followed in 1092. The Norman domination of Sicily inaugurated a period of peaceful prosperity, marked by artistic and cultural patronage of the highest order, particularly under King Roger II. The greatest surviving monuments from the period are the vast and richly decorated Cathedral and Palace of Palermo and the cathedrals of Monreale and Cefiti.

Edward the Confessor, king of England 1042–66, used his Norman connections to protect himself from the Godwin family. They were as wealthy as he was himself, and he named William of Normandy as his heir to bolster his own position. In the longer term, however, it gave William a claim to the English throne.

An ivory panel from the 6th-century throne of Bishop Maximian of Ravenna. The upper panel contains the Chi-Rho of Christ flanked by deer and peacocks, symbols of heavenly paradise. This was the central Christian message of hope proclaimed by John the Baptist (centre) and the four evangelists, pictured in the central panel below.

CHRISTIANITY AND SOCIETY

The conversion of the Roman emperor Constantine brought wealth, converts, and greater unity to the Christian religion, which had previously consisted of largely autonomous communities dotted around the Mediterranean rim. These transformations had turned the Church into a substantial but by no means monolithic entity by AD 500. The countryside was far from fully Christianized, and few missions had been mounted beyond the old Roman frontiers.

Between 500 and 1000, further missionary work, the development of more regular religious provision, and the transformation of its structures of authority combined to make Christianity the dominant religion of Europe.

Huge efforts were put into spreading the word, both into the countryside and more generally into non-Roman Europe. The populations of Ireland and Scotland embraced the Christian message in the 5th and 6th centuries; the Anglo-Saxons did so in the 7th; continental Germany up to the Elbe was converted in the 8th; the Slavs in the 9th and 10th centuries; and Scandinavia in the 10th and 11th centuries. Some points of resistance remained, particularly among the Elbe Slavs; however, by the start of the second Christian millennium the new religion was a dominating force across the map of Europe. The fundamental problem now facing Christian leaders was how to ensure adequate Christian provision across this huge expanse of territory. Missionary work was conducted by relatively small groups of priests and monks, and many individual missionaries, in order to minimize hostility among potential converts, incorporated as much as possible of pre-Christian religious beliefs and practice into their message. The result of this combination of toleration and a shortage of priests tended to be syncretism: local mixtures of pre- and Christian belief and practice. The situation only really began to be addressed in the Carolingian Renaissance. At that time, on the back of Charlemagne's power and prestige, the Christian scholars gathered at his court defined a core of necessary Christian learning and, through it, established for the first time general standards of piety and practice for monks, priests, and laymen. Trained manpower on a very large scale – many thousands per kingdom – was required to bring the reform programme to fruition, which was not achieved before the end of the millennium.

At the same time, Church structures and patterns of authority had been transformed beyond all recognition. Early medieval kings and emperors saw themselves as divinely appointed rulers. On this basis, they exercised power over Church institutions and resources, often with good intentions, but with an in-built tendency to fragment the Church by making its structures operate on a kingdom-by-kingdom basis. As the successors of St Peter, popes had long been acknowledged as the most senior of Western bishops. Between the 9th and the 11th centuries, however, the papacy reinvented itself, partly on the back of the central role Charlemagne had given it in the Carolingian Renaissance, to become a unifying force within Western Christendom. Ideological acceptance of its authority combined with the emergence of a Rome-centred canon law gave the Western Church a unity that, to a significant extent, operated independently of political boundaries. The price, however, was high. Popes had effectively claimed the kind of religious authority which Byzantine emperors considered their sole preserve. The resulting friction culminated in a definitive split between Greek East and Latin West in the Great Schism of 1054, when the Western Church definitively rejected Byzantine pretensions to hegemony over all Christians.

Christian Microcosms

Early medieval Christians believed they belonged to one religion. In practice, however, the fall of the Roman Empire halted the processes which had begun to generate real unity of practice, belief, and discipline, all of which depended upon the legal authority and financial support of the emperors. In fact, the early medieval Church was a loose association of regional units, despite continued papal claims to universal authority.

Structures of authority

Roman imperial collapse returned some early medieval Churches to the isolated position characteristic of early Christian communities under Roman persecution. The British Church, in particular, was left to itself, with very little contact with the continent from the mid-5th century. As a result, the British Church and the Irish Church which developed from it preserved many of the practices and doctrines of the Church of *c.*400 in fossilized form, while the rest of the Church continued to develop. When these Churches came back into contact with the Western mainstream in the late 6th century, their lack of hierarchically organized bishops and deviant views on the date of Easter caused serious problems.

The rest of the former Roman West was divided between successor kingdoms, the borders of which sometimes failed to correspond to those of the Church. In the early 500s, successive metropolitan

The 6th-century manual of John Climakos saw monks as climbing a long and narrow ladder to heaven, from which demons attempted to pull them back to earth. This image quickly took visual form, as in this 12th-century example from St Catherine's monastery on Mt Sinai.

bishops of Arles, located in Visigothic and then Ostrogothic territory, had suffragan bishops in the Burgundian kingdom. As a result of the cross-border contacts they maintained, they attracted accusations of disloyalty. In practice, Christianity largely functioned on a kingdom-by-kingdom basis, as kings appointed bishops and were unwilling to allow too much contact with other Churches in a world where political frontiers were still very fluid. The vigour of these functionally separate Churches varied. In 6th-century Gaul and 7th-century Spain, traditions were established of regular kingdom-wide ecclesiastical councils of bishops, called to deal with all kinds of issues: doctrinal, ceremonial, and organizational. The gathered bishops were aware of ancient Church practice and the previous decisions of their own councils, and coherent traditions of ecclesiastical evolution were established. These gatherings relied upon kings to call the councils and to help enforce their decisions, so that, as royal power grew and waned in effectiveness, so too did regional Church traditions rise and fall. As the kingdom of the Merovingian Franks collapsed in the 7th century, so did the coherence of the Frankish Church.

The papacy

The role of the papacy in the post-Roman period was extremely limited. In preceding centuries, the papacy had established its reputation as a bastion of orthodoxy, but the ability of individual popes to intervene in a set of events depended upon their location. In central and southern Italy, Sicily, and Sardinia, popes enjoyed full metropolitan powers. More than metropolitan bishops elsewhere, they could influence episcopal appointments and were also responsible for calling councils of subordinates and overseeing all doctrinal matters. Elsewhere, popes had no direct powers of appointment and little active influence. Because of the Roman See's prestige, some kings liked their leading bishop to receive the papal pallium, a woollen sash marking out the recipient as a special papal representative; however,

conversion of Roman emperors, which caused the Church to grow hugely in wealth and brought to an end martyrdom as a route for Christians to show particular devotion to their faith. Monasticism – often referred to as a "living martyrdom"– emerged as a replacement, for the most part originally in the form of individual asceticism and to satisfy those who felt that standards were slipping within the Church. This early period was characterized by extraordinary feats of endurance, such as those of St Antony, who lived in the Egyptian desert for 40 years, and St Symeon the Stylite, who lived on top of a pillar in Syria. By definition, therefore, early monasticism stood outside the mainstream Church and was sometimes overtly critical of it, even if bishops periodically attempted to assert their authority over the phenomenon.

In the 5th to 7th centuries, in the central areas of the West – Italy, France, and Spain – bishops to an extent brought the monastic movement under control. In particular, because of the dangers of excess and the arrogance of self-appointed authority inherent in individual asceticism, they worked to establish a communal form of monasticism. Under the new norms, the authority of a community's leader – the abbot – was strongly emphasized, monks were not allowed to move around as they pleased, and the pattern of life became generally moderate, involving reasonable amounts of food and a mixed day of labour, study, and prayer. By the 6th century, these norms were reflected, in different variants, in a cluster of rules related to the running of monastic life, such as The Rule of the Master and The Rule of St Benedict.

Even so, bishops were not generally able to interfere in the daily workings of these institutions, and monastic founders were able to control life as they chose. This allowed many local variations. In northern Europe, for instance, among the Franks and Anglo-Saxons, kings granted monastic land considerable tax relief. Local aristocrats quickly established family monasteries in response: these were effectively tax shelters where one could store surplus relatives who might otherwise have claimed a share of family land.

In western Britain and Ireland, cut off after 400, older, more individual ascetic traditions prevailed; when the two worlds came back into contact in the late 6th century, continental churchmen were suddenly confronted with great individual ascetics such as the Irish saint Columbanus. This determined ascetic made a huge impression, and he established abbeys in France and Italy, and a stringently austere set of rules. Not only did the regional Churches of individual kingdoms function in largely separate fashion in the early Middle Ages, therefore, but so, too, did the monasteries.

St Symeon the Stylite's self-denial of all material comforts and even human companionship won huge admiration from the flocks of pilgrims who came to Qu'alat Siman in Syria both during his lifetime and after his death. The remains of the pilgrim hostels, three huge pilgrimage churches, and even the bottom portion of his pillar can still be seen there today.

popes could demand little in return. Popes also remained a potential court of final appeal for difficult cases involving churchmen, but the costs of travel and unwillingness of kings to allow issues to pass outside their borders meant that few appeals were made. The one region of the West with a closer relationship to the papacy was Anglo-Saxon England. Much of the evangelization of this country was conducted by the Roman mission sent by Pope Gregory I in 597, and close ties continued. Popes occasionally even supplied Archbishops of Canterbury, of whom the most significant was Theodore of Tarsus (archbishop from 668–90). Within his episcopate, the entire English Church was reorganized and its standards brought into line with the best of current continental practice.

Monasticism

Monastic endeavour during this period was also characterized by similarly fragmented patterns. Monasticism originally emerged as a response to the

The Christianization of Europe

Roman imperial power spread the Christian religion as far north as Hadrian's Wall in the north of England, and up to the rivers Rhine and Danube by the end of the 5th century. Over the next 500 years, missionary heroes would spread Christianity to the Arctic Circle and as far east as the river Volga.

This 12th-century illustration to the Chronicle *of John Scylitzes portrays the epoch-making moment when an embassy from King Vladimir of Kiev arrived in Constantinople to receive formal instruction in Christianity from the Patriarch. The king's conversion was quickly followed by that of the Russian elites, and marked the birth of Orthodox Holy Russia.*

Northern Europe

Early medieval sources preserve the names of many individual missionaries of the period. One of the first victories for the Christian faith came in Ireland, where, from the early 5th century, St Patrick made many converts. Much of the missionary work in Ireland was carried out by British missionaries, their efforts supplemented by missionaries from Roman Gaul such as Palladius. The Irish Church, through individual ascetics such as Columba and Ninian, was then responsible for spreading Christianity into Scotland. In 597, Pope Gregory I sent a Roman mission under St Augustine of Canterbury to Anglo-Saxon England, where Aethelbert, king of Kent and overlord of much of southern England, had married a Christian Frankish princess. His conversion made him the first Anglo-Saxon king. This papal initiative was supplemented by the efforts of more Irish missionaries, such as the brothers Cedd and Chad, who in the early 6th century moved from Scotland into England. The last pagan Anglo-Saxon realm, on the Isle of Wight, was converted by armed intervention in 682.

Christian missionary work in the Low Countries and northern Germany began in the 8th century. The Anglo-Saxon missionary Boniface was instrumental, particularly in Frisia, until his martyrdom in 754; however, it was the Carolingians who carried the work to fruition. Between 772 and 804, Charlemagne imposed Christianity upon the pagan Saxons, and his son Louis was responsible for the first attempts to convert Scandinavia through the efforts of St Anskar in 830 and 845. It was not until the mid-10th century, however – with King Harold Bluetooth – that large-scale success followed.

The conversion of the Slavs

Much of the conversion of the Slavs to Christianity was accomplished by Western missionaries. Successive Archbishops of Salzburg in the south, receiving considerable financial and military assistance from Frankish kings, organized the 9th-century conversions of Bohemia and Moravia. Further north, Otto I established a series of bishoprics east of the Elbe under control of a new archbishopric at Magdeburg in the 10th century, and his grandson Otto III established a separate Polish Church under its own archbishop at Gniezno. For the Elbe Slavs, however, the association with imperial domination was too strong. They rejected Christianity in the great rebellion of 983 and did not return to it until the 12th century. These Western efforts were periodically supplemented by Byzantine missions. In the 860s, the Moravians requested missionaries from the Byzantine Empire because they again perceived Frankish Christianity as an instrument of Carolingian domination. This led two brothers, Cyril and Methodius, with papal blessing, to journey north, where they famously created the first written version of a Slavic tongue – Glagolithic – into which they translated the Gospels and other religious texts. Frankish pressure caused the expulsion of Methodius after Cyril's death

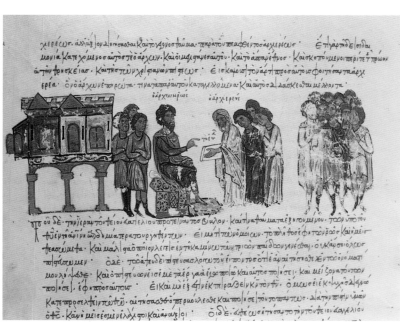

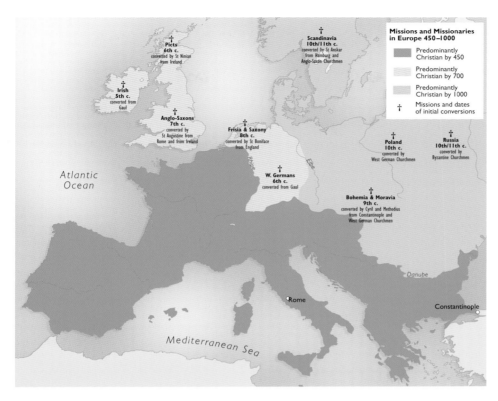

Missions and Missionaries in Europe 450–1000

- Predominantly Christian by 450
- Predominantly Christian by 700
- Predominantly Christian by 1000
- † Missions and dates of initial conversions

Picts
6th c.
converted by St Ninian
from Ireland

Irish
5th c.
converted from
Gaul

Anglo-Saxons
7th c.
converted by
St Augustine from
Rome and from Ireland

Frisia & Saxony
8th c.
converted by St Boniface
from England

Scandinavia
10th/11th c.
converted by St Anskar
from Hamburg and
Anglo-Saxon Churchmen

Poland
10th c.
converted by
West German Churchmen

Russia
10th/11th c.
converted by
Byzantine Churchmen

W. Germans
6th c.
converted from Gaul

Bohemia & Moravia
9th c.
converted by Cyril and Methodius
from Constantinople and
West German Churchmen

Atlantic Ocean

Rhine
Elbe
Danube

Rome

Constantinople

Mediterranean Sea

By c.450, Christianity had spread to the frontiers of the Roman Empire, even if it was still a substantially urban phenomenon. This map shows the subsequent spread of Christianity northwards and eastwards during the rest of the millennium, from the British Isles by c.700, to Poland, Scandinavia, and Russia by c.1050. These dates mark the formal conversion of the elite, and a long process of Christianization was to follow before the religion was established in all strata of the European population.

in 869, but their legacy flourished in Macedonia, from where the Bulgarian Empire was converted in the 880s. In the next century, the Kievan Rus were also converted under Byzantine influence, when first Olga and then her son Prince Vladimir accepted the faith. With this conversion, the majority of Slavic-speaking Europe had become nominally Christian.

Christianity and the countryside

The Christianization of Europe was not accomplished merely by converting royal houses and baptizing their subjects. Such acts only declared an intention. Church leaders also needed to bring notionally converted populations to a fuller Christian observance, spreading knowledge of the faith and providing the priests and churches that would make it possible for populations to lead fully Christian lives. Until that happened, the missionary situation characteristically generated syncretism: local mixtures of new Christian and old pagan practice and belief. In some places, too – as was famously recommended by Pope Gregory I to Abbot Mellitus on the latter's journey to Anglo-Saxon England in 597 – churchmen deliberately retained what they could of pagan cultic practice to minimize any hostility to their new religion.

The challenge of converting the north required substantial structural changes to a religion that had grown up in the urban Mediterranean. Early Christianity had customarily limited preaching to bishops only, to preserve purity of teaching. This worked in the Mediterranean where the majority of the population lived in towns and could gather in one place. In the larger, rural dioceses of the north, however, this meant that far fewer people could hear a sermon at any one time. Hence Bishop Caesarius of Arles began to license priests to preach in the 520s, and the new custom was generally adopted over the next two generations. Northern bishops also began to create rural chapels in their dioceses. By the 590s, there were 40 such rural chapels in the diocese of Tours alone, and, in areas such as these, Christianity was evolving a parish system, with a priest and church in every rural community. At this stage, as has been well documented in Anglo-Saxon England, rural priests probably lived at one central place and worked in teams, visiting the communities in their charge only periodically. By such means, Christianity began to adapt to the challenges of the north, but much remained to be done. The quality of Christian observance depended ultimately on the quality of the priesthood charged with transmitting the religion, and here, as late as the 8th century, matters varied greatly. As well as leading the mission to Frisia, Boniface also encountered Frankish bishops with very dubious beliefs. It was only in the Carolingian period that higher general standards of religious observance began to be set for the clergy, and, through them, to reach the population at large.

700–1000

THE RISE OF THE WEST

THE CHRISTIANIZATION OF EUROPE **31**

The Carolingian Renaissance

The Carolingian Renaissance witnessed a general revival in the teaching of Latin in Western Europe, but only as a means to an end. Firmly believing that his victories were the result of God's favour, Charlemagne was determined to reform the Church. He was particularly concerned that the clergy's poor Latin had led to the corruption of Biblical texts and service books, so that incorrect doctrines were being taught.

Learning

Charlemagne was also concerned that, without adequate Latin, religious services were losing their efficacy. This thinking was ritualistic, in that only "correct" religious performance would have the desired effect with God. To address the problem, Charlemagne gathered at his court the leading scholars of his day and the best late-Roman teaching texts, such as the grammars of Donatus and Priscian. Their texts on Latin grammar had been written centuries before and were the standard texts throughout the Middle Ages. Men and texts combined to re-create a tradition, and from *c.*800, classical Latin became the standard language of educated churchmen. Charlemagne also set his scholars to produce "correct" texts of all the vital religious works. Pope

Hadrian was approached for the best available copies of holy books, which provided the starting point. Among others, Alcuin from Northumbria set to work to reconstruct the "true" text of the Bible from the four Latin traditions currently in circulation, and Paul the Deacon, from Italy, worked to produce a standard service book. Others concentrated upon canon law. The new set texts – with an apparatus of Latin grammars and literature, Biblical commentary, and wider theological reflection – became part of a new standard collection of materials necessary for any educated churchman.

With the emperor's backing, this new stock library of Latin Christianity was disseminated to all the major monasteries within Charlemagne's domains – such as St Riquier, Gall, Lorsch, and Tours – and established the basic curriculum of medieval learning. In the process, much classical literature, considered useful for learning Latin or for the information it contained, was preserved, but much also was lost. Few pre-Carolingian manuscripts survive; anything the Carolingians did not find useful was thrown away and forever lost.

At heart, then, the Carolingian intellectual effort was preservative rather than creative, although, even in its first generation, the assembled scholars competed with each other to attract Charlemagne's favour through a very vigorous court poetry. In subsequent generations, however, more creative work followed in every field: history, theology, and astronomy, among many others.

Christian observance

Charlemagne always intended his intellectuals to contribute to a wider reform of Christian observance. Characteristic of his reign were general statements, such as the *Admonitio Generalis* of 789, which combined general urgings for a holier life for everyone with long lists of more precise measures. To turn big words into practical action, the emperor organized reforming synods throughout his domains in the 800s. These were impressively practical occasions, with reforming bishops setting targets for improve-

Carolingian kings recycled wealth in vast quantities to their flagship monastic foundations, in thanks for the victories that they ascribed to divine intervention. A characteristic feature of the great monastic cathedrals was their imposing western façades. That of Corvey in Germany (built between 873 and 886) is one of the few to survive largely intact.

ment for the local clergy that reflected their current situations. A much simpler set of improvements was laid out east in Metz, for instance, than in the old Christian centre of Orléans.

A similar approach was also taken to monasticism under Louis the Pious. Between 817 and 820, further reforming councils defined a standard form of monasticism, based on the Rule of St Benedict as revised by Benedict of Aniane in the late 8th century, and urged it upon all existing monastic houses. The new standard demanded a complete separation of monasteries from secular influence, the centralized direction of all their landed assets, and a life devoted to prayer and study.

The effects of all this are hard to judge. Few monasteries immediately adopted the new reform, and it was to be centuries before even Western clergymen generally conformed to the new standards set for them, let alone their parishioners. For the first time, however, efforts had been made to enforce a definition of the levels of Christian piety appropriate to laymen, monks, and clergy throughout Western Christendom. As the Carolingians lost power in the later 9th century, so, too, was lost their ability to turn ambition into practice; however, an overall vision had been established that would later be brought to fruition by the medieval papacy.

Art and architecture

Charlemagne's astonishing military and territorial victories brought a huge amount of wealth into his hands, and substantial sums were recycled for artistic endeavour of all kinds. In painting, as reflected in manuscript illumination, there was a decisive shift back towards classical models. The richly coloured pictures of the *Coronation Gospels* of Charlemagne's own time and the narrative pen and ink drawings of the Utrecht Psalter (*c*.830) both rejected the abstract, and they seem to have drawn directly on now lost classical exemplars. Although other works were not quite as classical in style, there was no continuation of the abstract Hiberno-Saxon style seen in post-Roman Britain.

Exquisite work was also achieved in fields such as ivory and metalwork. The most impressive body of surviving evidence, however, relates to architecture: palace complexes and, particularly, churches. Here, as Charlemagne's surviving palatine chapel at Aachen shows, there was some experimentation with Byzantine-style domed structures, but the basilica became the basic form of Carolingian architecture. The great monastery church at Fulda was based on the basilica of Old St Peter's in Rome, which also influenced other great constructions such as the churches built at St Riquier and advocated in the Plan of St Gall. The latter was not actually built, but the plan itself was highly influential. This design for an idealized monastery was created in accordance with the rules for monastic life as laid out by St Benedict. It illustrates a great three-aisled basilica with apses at both the western and the traditional eastern end – a Carolingian innovation – and six towers, placed three at each end. Although the decline of the Carolingians reduced the amount of wealth available for grand building programmes in the second half of the 9th century, nonetheless the first, crucial steps towards Romanesque architecture were taken in the elaborate basilicas constructed under their aegis.

The Carolingian Renaissance extended into most fields of artistic endeavour. This ivory book cover, carved in realistic high relief, portrays the Archangel Michael slaying the dragon as described in the Book of Revelation. *It was produced in the Rhineland in the early 9th century.*

Redefining the Papacy

Early popes claimed to be the successors of St Peter, but enjoyed little real power. The Emperor Charlemagne, however, regularly sought papal rulings on religious disputes, bringing the papacy a new centrality in the Latin Church by the early 9th century. Over the next two centuries, papal authority over canon law, and the prestige derived from its sponsorship of monastic reform, turned old ideological claims into practical power.

Popes and Carolingians

From the mid-8th century, popes turned to the Carolingian rulers of Francia, first as kings then as emperors, for temporal support as Byzantine power in Italy ebbed away and Lombard power increased. A series of armed Frankish interventions first halted Lombard acquisitions of papal territory, and, when Charlemagne finally conquered the Lombard kingdom in 774, he gave Pope Hadrian full temporal control of a designated body of lands: the Papal States. For their part, the popes provided political and religious legitimacy to the new imperial house of the West. The first Carolingian king Pepin I's acquisition of monarchical power was formally approved by Pope Zacharias in 751, and Charlemagne's imperial coronation was conducted by Pope Leo in Rome. More generally, Charlemagne always sought advice and uncorrupted sacred texts from the papal see in attempting his Church reforms.

Canon law

The Carolingians' use of the papacy established the general custom among Western churchmen of turning to Rome for advice on non-doctrinal matters. Also from the 9th century, new developments in canon law greatly developed papal authority. Canon law had been built up slowly from a variety of sources: Old and New Testament extracts, the writings of church fathers, and collected decisions of church councils. In the late and post-Roman periods, the church council was the main mechanism for amplifying old rulings and dealing with new problems, but this had tended to generate fragmentation when the successor states' churches largely operated as separate conciliar bodies. Papal letters had always been considered a possible source of canon law; however, because of the Carolingian's use of the papacy, they became, from the 9th century, the only generally acknowledged source of authoritative new rulings. Old materials were retained, but new problems – doctrinal and practical – were increasingly referred to the papacy, and papal letters increasingly dominated canon law collections. Strikingly, papal letters had become, by *c.*850, the key documents to forge. The greatest canon law forgery was the *Pseudo-Isidorean Decretals*, which was compiled in later 9th-century Francia to protect the rights of suffragan bishops against the interference of their metropolitans and proclaimed the rights of popes over all secular rulers. It contained the forged *Donation of Constantine*, purporting that Constantine had left his throne to the pope. All its important forgeries took the form of supposed papal letters.

Monastic reform

Ideological acceptance of this general increase in papal authority was generated by the role popes played in continuing monastic reform. Moves to de-secularize Western monasteries began under the Carolingians, with their imperial power used to override local interests. With the collapse of the dynasty, this strategy lost impetus, but interest in its reformed Benedictine observance remained strong among Western clerics. The necessary support to override local secular interests was obtained, therefore, by a new route: negotiating simultaneously with the regional secular lords who replaced Carolingian emperors and with popes. Papal protection thus became a characteristic mark of the new reformed monastic federations. The most famous of these grew up around Cluny in Burgundy, but there were others: in the Rhineland around the monastery of Gorze, in Rome itself, and in other centres further north, such as the foundations of William of Volpiano in Flanders. The whole ideology of Benedictine reform centred on the separation of the Church from secular interests, and this ideology became increasingly influential as monks from the reformed houses were promoted to the episcopate by regional rulers who accepted the legitimacy of this new vision of Christianity. Over time, this again promoted the papal profile, as the upper echelons of the different regional sections of the Western Church were increasingly populated by men who considered that the Church ought to be a more separate entity than had their forbears of previous centuries and who saw the pope as the champion and practical head of this independent body.

The creation of Western Christendom

Further impetus was added to the general reforming ideology centring on the papacy by the Ottonians, who consistently appointed reform- minded churchmen from northern Europe to Italian positions in the 10th century. In the 11th century, this bore unexpected fruit in the doctrines of papal monarchy developed in the circles of Pope Leo IX and Gregory VII. From monastic reform, they took the idea that Church and State should be separate. Secular rulers did not have the right to appoint men to high positions in the Church, whose head was really the pope. Canon law, now to be updated only by papal decision thanks to the Carolingian legacy, provided

the practical vehicle by which that headship could be expressed.

Journeys to Rome remained expensive, and the Church controlled too much landed wealth for kings ever to be willing to lose all control over its senior appointments. The practical everyday involvement of the pope in the affairs of regional Churches everywhere from Scotland to Poland was nonetheless accomplished by other means. Papal authority was brought to the regions, not via the pope in person, but in the form of collected and carefully edited editions of papal decisions – manuals of canon law – the strictures of which were applied by local judges whose courts got their authority from papal appointment. This mechanism required several centuries for its full evolution, and regional Churches were never fully extracted from the interference of their kings, but the foundations of the medieval and modern papacy were securely laid.

Charlemagne considered that God had made him emperor to reform the Christian Church, and that the papacy existed to assist him. The papal view, that the emperor was in fact their subordinate, eventually prevailed, however. The stock image become one of Leo III crowning a submissive Charlemagne, as here. This difference pointed the way towards the ideological claims of the Papal monarchs of the high Middle Ages.

Iconoclasm and the East–West Divide

In the late Roman period, Greek churchmen, operating through the Patriarchate of Constantinople, had largely set the agenda defining the evolution of Christianity. For the first time, however, Western churchmen threw off this domination in the iconoclast dispute of the 8th century. Over the next two centuries, the papacy's refusal to toe an Eastern line eventually generated a formal split between Rome and Constantinople.

The iconoclast dispute

Byzantine state ideology held that the Empire had been created by God and that emperors were chosen by God to rule with Him on earth. Such an ideology created respect for the imperial office, but meant that disasters, such as the 7th-century Arab conquests, were bound to result in religious self-examination. Why was God punishing his chosen people? In the early 8th century, Byzantine emperors and churchmen concluded that icons – pictures of saints, the Virgin, and Christ – were the problem. In *c.*725, Leo III decreed that they broke the Second Commandment and were leading the people into idolatry: the reason for God's manifest anger. Icons

An 11th-century icon of St Peter. Emperor Leo III decreed c.725 that worship of images was idolatrous and that all icons should be destroyed. By 843, icon worship was re-established, however – the Church had triumphed over the emperor.

were a natural scapegoat because, in the late 680s, the Emperor Justinian II, for the first time ever, used an actual image of Christ on his coinage and, at the same moment, reopened the war against Islam. The Islamic world reacted by definitively rejecting all forms of figurative art (the change, to judge by Islamic coins, coming precisely in the 690s), and Justinian lost heavily. God had made His position on icons clear.

The destruction of icons aroused some hostility within Byzantium, particularly among monks, who used them in their devotions. For believers, icons captured the essence of the holy men and women they pictured. They opened a "window into heaven" and could induce the saint to use his or her power on the petitioner's behalf. They varied in size from great wall paintings to small handheld medallions, and were used to cure everything from life-threatening diseases to illiteracy. Leo's choice seemed to be justified, however, by the return of stability to the Islamic front. In the 740s, the Abbasids overthrew the Umayyads, and the capital moved from Syria to Baghdad in Iraq, shifting the centre of gravity of the Islamic world. This reduced Byzantium to a very peripheral concern and eased the military pressure exerted upon it. The First Iconoclasm came to an end, therefore, only late in the 8th century, when the Empress Irene called the second Council of Nicaea in 787, which duly lifted the ban on figurative religious art. But more military disasters followed, this time administered by the Bulgurs under their Khagan Krum, who killed the Emperor Nicephorus I in 811. Because of this, iconoclasm was restored under Leo V in 815; however, this time, its association with victory was broken by further disasters, especially the loss of the key fortress of Amorium to Muslim forces. In 843, in the Restoration of Orthodoxy – a formal ceremony on the first Sunday of Lent held in the cathedral of Hagia Sophia in Constantinople – iconoclasm was definitively rejected by the Greek Church.

Within Christendom as a whole, iconoclasm had some very broad ramifications. Its initial adoption was condemned by churchmen from Syria to Ireland, and its failure to win over wider Christian opinion was one reason why Irene rescinded it in 787. By this stage, however, a triumphant Charlemagne already had his eyes on the imperial title and was ready to use even the restoration of images as an occasion to criticize Byzantine pretensions to Christian leadership. Where Pope Hadrian accepted the decrees of the second Council of Nicaea with enthusiasm, Charlemagne's Frankish Church in the Synod of Frankfurt of 794 argued that Byzantine policy on images was still erroneous, as they were placing them too much at the heart of worship. This was part of a general attack on Byzantine pretensions that their emperor ruled "with God".

Filioque and the Great Schism

Once Charlemagne had secured his imperial title and Byzantine recognition – granted by Michael I in 812 – Carolingian religious criticism of Byzantium sub-sided. By the middle of the 9th century, however, an alternative and rising religious power in the West, the papacy, was becoming self-assertive enough to engage in outright criticism of the Byzantine Church for its own purposes. None of the issues was insoluble in itself, but, when the general context demanded it, they together formed the basis of a periodically fierce hostility. In the 860s, Pope Nicholas I took the Patriarch Photius of Constantinople to task on three points. The pope had sponsored a Latin mission to Bulgaria, but Photius maintained that the Bulgarians "belonged" to the Greek East. Nicholas was also personally critical of Photius as a political appointee of the Byzantine Emperor Michael III. Thirdly, East and West disagreed over the wording of the Creed. In the West, from the third Council of Toledo in 589, the custom had developed of adding the words "and the Son" (*filioque*) to the standard Creed of Nicaea-Constantinople, where it talked about the "procession" of the Holy Spirit. In the Carolingian period, as part of Charlemagne's reform of Christian observance, it became customary for the Creed to be chanted during the Mass, which generalized the habit. The Eastern Church maintained the original wording of the Creed, which talked of procession only from the Father.

Such hostilities were not consistently maintained, and, in the 10th century, with the rise of the Ottonians and their influence over the papacy, some of the heat was taken out of the disputes. Otto II married a Byzantine princess, and all the Ottos respected Byzantine interests in Italy, so that relations between East and West were generally good. From the early 11th century, as reforming Western churchmen developed ever stronger ideas of papal leadership, however, hostilities were resumed on a series of fronts.

Politically, in the early 1050s, the papacy switched its backing from the Byzantines to the intrusive Normans in southern Italy. *Filioque* remained an issue, and, as part of their general rejection of the claims of kings and emperors to have control over the Church, popes were ready to act aggressively towards the imperially appointed Eastern Patriarchs. When Michael Cerularius sent letters on his accession demanding recognition as "oecumenical [general or senior] Patriarch", Leo IX responded by demanding that the Roman see be recognized as "head and mother of the Church" ("*caput et mater ecclesiarum*"). Mutual excommunications followed in 1054, and the Great Schism was born. Within it, various doctrinal and disciplinary issues were significant, but, at heart, it was the product of Western self-assertion against Eastern pretensions to religious hegemony, in an era when secular control of the Church was being rejected.

The extinction of Carolingians freed the Papacy from the rival religious claims of a Western imperial dynasty, but the Patriarchate of Constantinople remained under the control of Byzantine emperors, who claimed to be the heads of Christendom. This underlying rivalry expressed itself in a range of disputes, and came to a head in Leo IX's excommunication of Michael Cerularius, here pictured in a 15th-century Greek manuscript, which inaugurated the Great Schism.

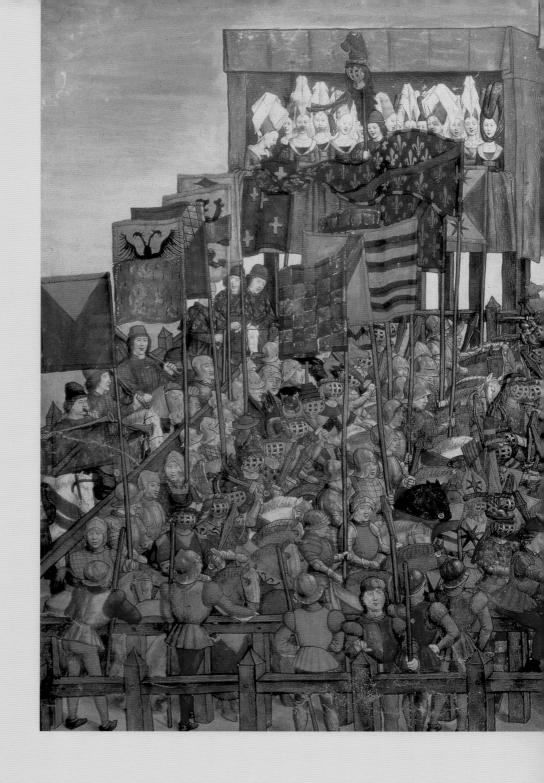

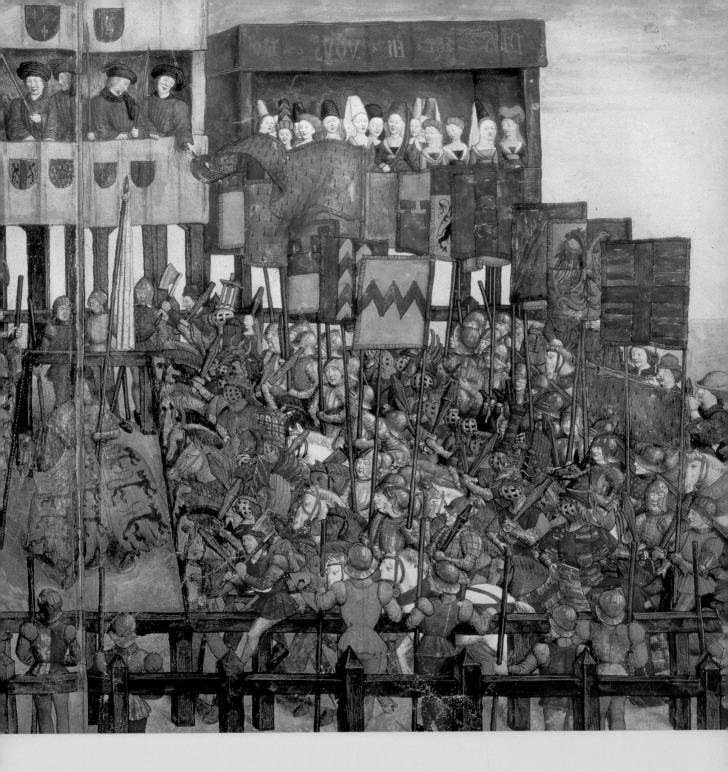

THE MIDDLE AGES

1000–1400

POLITICS AND GOVERNMENT

1095–9 First Crusade launched by Pope Urban II at Clermont in November 1095. It recaptures Jerusalem at a terrible cost. Crusader states are established at Jerusalem, Antioch, and Tripoli.

1066 William Duke of Normandy defeats Harold of Wessex, the last Anglo-Saxon king, at the Battle of Hastings.

1209–26 The Albigensian Crusades attempt to stamp out the Cathar heresy in the Languedoc.

1201–4 Fourth Crusade, culminating in the sack of Constantinople by Western forces.

1190–2 Third Crusade is a qualified success for Westerners.

1183 The Peace of Constance. The Lombard League recognizes imperial overlordship.

1167 The towns of northern Italy form the Lombard League in defiance of Frederick Barbarossa's imperial claims.

1146–8 Second Crusade fails to recapture Edessa from Zengi, Atabeg of Mosul.

1000　　　　　**1062**　　　　　**1125**　　　　　**1187**

SOCIETY AND CULTURE

1049 At the Council of Rheims Pope Leo IX condemns priests and bishops who have paid for their appointments, beginning a high-profile programme of reform focusing on lay interference in ecclesiastical matters.

1054 Schism between Western and Eastern Churches, triggered by a dispute over the precise wording of the Creed.

1073 Popular acclaim in Rome sweeps Cardinal Hildebrand to the papal throne as Gregory VII.

1098 Robert of Molesmes founds a monastery at Citeaux. It becomes the home of the new Cistercian order.

1119 Foundation of the Knights Templar in Jerusalem.

1137–51 Abbot Suger begins a massive rebuilding of the Abbey Church of St Denis in a new, light, ambitious style later derided as Gothic.

1194 Beginning of the rebuilding of Chartres Cathedral.

1200 Grant of charter to the University of Paris by Philip I.

1215 Magna Carta. The charter confirms the liberties of the English Church and sets out the barons' feudal duties to the monarch.

1357 Start of the peasant revolts across Europe. The most notable are in France and and England. Known as the *jacqueries* in France, the rebels burnt and pillaged castles massacring the inhabitants. The rebellion was put down violently. The peasants revolt starting in 1381 in England claims to champion the rights of the rural poor.

1307–14 Trial of the Knights Templar results in their abolition and the public burning of their grand master.

1337–1453 The Hundred Years War, a convenient label for protracted hostilities resulting from the rival claims of England and France. Both countries are forced to revolutionize their taxation and administration systems.

50 | **1312** | **1375** | **1400**

1274 Death of St Thomas Aquinas. His *Summa Theologica* was the most influential work of Christian philosophy of the Middle Ages.

1321 Death of Dante Alighieri. His *Divine Comedy* offers the single most complete snapshot of life and thought in 13th and 14th century Europe.

1309 Clement V takes the papacy into exile at Avignon.

1348–9 Black Death ravages Europe, killing at least one fifth of the population.

1351 Boccacio completes *The Decameron*, a tale of 10 travellers taking refuge from the Black Death.

1377 Return of the papacy to Rome under Gregory IX. Later in the year two rival claimants are acclaimed as pope beginning almost 40 years of schism. The schism will finally come to an end in 1514 with the Council of Constance.

*c.*1260 The Polo family begin their travels in the Mongol Empire. Beginning of paper manufacture at Fabriano.

52 Florence and Genoa strike their own gold florins.

The 14th-century Siennese painter
Duccio here depicts the temptation of
Christ on the mountain. He draws upon
a common medieval theme, the snares
of worldly power. Perhaps appropriately,
he was working in one of the greatest
commercial cities of his age.

THE SHAPE OF MEDIEVAL EUROPE

The authors of the chronicles, letters and treaties that shape our perception of medieval Europe were almost always untypical; their works may be as misleading as they are evocative. Far fewer people believed that the world was flat than we might imagine, yet the period remains a strange landscape in which the familiar is surrounded by the alien.

The cathedrals and mosques, mosaics and minarets that map out today's tourist trail are the legacy of a political geography a millennium old. From the early 8th century onwards, the western and southern shores of the Mediterranean belonged to the Islamic Empire. Byzantium and Islam had contested its eastern shores since the 7th century, while its northern shores were divided between Byzantium and the West. By the 10th century, Islam was no longer an empire but a series of caliphates. It is easy, however, to exaggerate its fragmentation: more than one of the pieces were larger than the empire of Charlemagne. From the 9th to the 13th centuries, the Russian princes of the "Rus" dynasty ruled a great empire covering most of Russia in Europe. Between Russia and Germany lay the Baltic peoples, still pagan and relatively independent of German or Christian influence. The 10th century had been the heyday of Scandinavian influence. For a time in the 11th century, one Viking, Cnut, had ruled in Denmark, England, Norway, and parts of Sweden.

Between Islam, Byzantium, Russia, and Scandinavia, the shape of Western Europe was defined. In the 9th century, the empire of Charlemagne had fragmented into three: the western fragment corresponded roughly to France; the eastern roughly to Germany. The middle comprised Lorraine, Provence, Burgundy, and much of Italy. In 1000, it was a collection of kingdoms and principalities; those to the south were often subject to anarchy or violent take-over bids; those to the north were usually part of Germany. In 1100, the corners of Christendom were all held by Normans: England, Sicily, southern Italy, and parts of Spain and Byzantium. The Norman kings of England could claim lordship over the duchy of Normandy in France.

Their successors, the Angevins, claimed an even wider lordship extending to Anjou and Aquitaine. In this period, the Baltic, which divided lowland Germany and Denmark, was far more of a frontier than the English channel.

Three large linguistic groups dominated Europe then as now: the western and southern Romance languages, descendants of Latin; the Germanic languages of the north; and the Slavonic languages of the east. A wealth of distinct tongues can be identified within each of these groups, not to mention many local dialects. It is very difficult to know precisely which languages and dialects were mutually intelligible. As is suggested by the 25 or more sub-dialects of modern Basque, for instance, it is likely that static societies produced quite isolated dialects that would sound alien even to the ears of a visitor from just over the horizon.

The Shape of Medieval Europe c.AD 1000

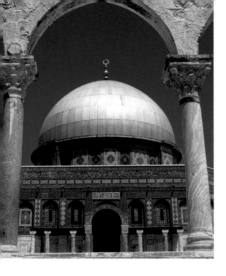

The Two Roman Empires

In AD 1000, the imperial mantle of Rome was claimed by two empires – Byzantium and the Holy Roman Empire. Although culturally and spiritually divorced, they shared many formative experiences. Both had been and continued to be shaped by forces outside Christendom – Vikings, Magyars, Mongols, and Turks – and both faced similar challenges to imperial authority from within their own borders.

Built on a site holy to all three monotheistic religions, the Dome of the Rock in Jerusalem was the meeting point of empires. Jerusalem had been transferred from Christian to Muslim hands in 638. This seismic event, more than any other, shaped the political geography of medieval Europe.

In the period between the accession of Basil I in 867 and the death of Basil II in 1025, Byzantium reached its zenith. In 880, Basil I retook lands in southern Italy. In the 10th century, successive campaigns recovered Syria, Cyprus, Crete, Cilicia, and parts of Mesopotamia and brought the Bulgars to terms. By the time of the death of Alexius I Comnenus in 1118, much in the east had been lost to Islam.

The Holy Roman Empire

In 962, the king of Germany, Otto the Great, was crowned Holy Roman Emperor by the pope. The empire of Charlemagne was long gone, and the frontier between what is now known as France and Germany was on the way to becoming the most conspicuous political boundary within Western Christendom. The imperial title had no precise political significance, although it did carry great prestige. The German emperors saw themselves as, variously, the apex of Christian society, the heirs of Charlemagne, and rulers of the Kingdom of Burgundy and of the Italian peninsula. In the early part of this period, they defended their right to be crowned in Rome and thus determine the holder of the papacy. Yet despite all of these claims and pretensions, the duchies that made up the kingdom were based on traditional and deep-rooted divisions between peoples, and they were reluctant to accept a higher level of authority.

Frederick Barbarossa

The career of Emperor Frederick Barbarossa demonstrates the peculiar dynamic that dominated medieval German politics. The nephew of the previous emperor, Conrad III (1137–52), he was elected by the German nobles in preference to Conrad's son, largely because he was directly descended from both of the two great warring family factions of German politics. In 1155, he marched into northern Italy, retrieving Ancona and Spoletto from their Norman conquerors, and, despite opposition, Frederick was crowned emperor by Pope Hadrian IV. The next year he married Beatrice, heir to the throne of Burgundy, and was acclaimed "father of his country". By 1157, however, an old argument had been rekindled: Hadrian claimed to have conferred the Empire on Frederick, whereas Barbarossa maintained that it had never been his to give. When Hadrian died in 1159, two claimants to the papacy arose: Alexander III was proclaimed pope in Rome, while Frederick, whether in

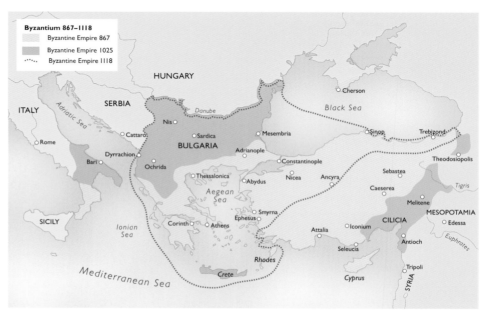

ignorance, guile, or earnest, proclaimed his own "imperialist" candidate, the anti-pope Victor IV. This provided a pretext for certain German princes to voice their discontent, and from then on Frederick could not rely on unanimous support for his Italian ventures. The towns of northern Italy seized upon the papal cause as justification for denying Frederick's claims of overlordship. In 1168, the newly united towns built a city at the junction of the Tanaro and Bormida to keep Frederick on his side of the Alps; they called it Alessandria, after Alexander III.

Although the ensuing 20 years were beset by defeat, victory, and compromise, Frederick only saw his role as that of emperor. The kingdoms of Burgundy and Italy were not "foreign"; the journeys to Rome were not merely for display; the settlements with German nobles were not "concessions". All three fell within his orbit of imperial power. It is perhaps fitting that Frederick died on crusade – those sorry expeditions epitomized the universalist aspirations of Christendom and the huge difficulties faced by those who sought to realize them.

The Byzantine Empire

In 1204, Constantinople fell to the Fourth Crusade. This single, shattering event colours all too easily the way in which we view Byzantine society in the first two centuries of the second millennium. It should be remembered that this Eastern Roman Empire survived the Western by a thousand years to become the longest-lived human empire after those of the Chinese and Egyptians. At the time of the death of Emperor Basil II (963–1025), Byzantium was the greatest power in the Mediterranean and Near East, and its capital the most glittering city. Its culture and learning were at the forefront of the European experience, but the history of Byzantine politics is characterized by senseless intrigue. Several dynasties vied for the throne, and Byzantium's political life was dominated by two powerful groups: the military aristocracy and the court officials. Basil II had kept both under control, but, when he died, the warlords proceeded to gather more and more of the Empire into their own hands. To compound problems, disputes over a minor technicality of doctrine led to a breakdown in ecclesiastical relations between East and West such that, in 1054, the pope excommunicated the spiritual leader of the Orthodox Church, the patriarch of Constantinople.

Alexius I Comnenus

It is telling that 13 emperors held office in the half-century following the death of Basil II in 1025. The coup and subsequent accession of Alexius I Comnenus (1081–1118) introduced a new dynasty to the throne and a new vigour to Byzantine military

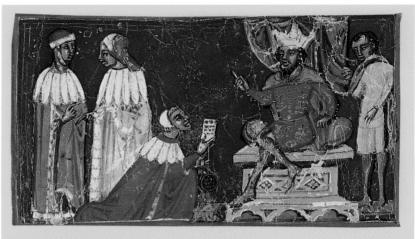

Frederick Barbarossa

The most striking example of Frederick Barbarossa's understanding of imperial authority was his elevation of Duke Vladislav II of Bohemia to the rank of king in 1158. Creating a king, and therefore a kingdom, where there had not been one before was a serious business. Previously, when Pepin the Short had sought to become first king of the Franks in the mid-8th century, he had secured the pope's aid in advance. Pope Hadrian IV had equally strong views on the extent and limits of imperial power, and in 1155 had refused to crown Frederick emperor until he had shown due reverence, and held the pope's bridle as though a vassal of the Holy Father. Hadrian would have recalled that Charlemagne himself received the title Roman Emperor from Pope Leo III, but Frederick knew that Charlemagne had then turned his back on Rome. Here, Frederick is shown receiving a papal legate. We can imagine that the exchange was heated.

and diplomatic activity. His life is celebrated in one of the most enjoyable of medieval biographies, the *Alexiad*, written by his daughter, Anna Comnena. For all her enthusiastic eulogizing of her father, Anna really did have something to boast about.

In the early 1080s, Alexius' most formidable enemy was the Norman Robert Guiscard, overlord by conquest of southern Italy and Sicily, and an opportunist of genius whose European ambitions seemingly knew no limit. Alexius, short of soldiers and cash, allied himself with Venice and brought to a halt Guiscard's eastern forays. Next, Alexius was threatened by the Patzinaks, a semi-barbarian horde settled to his north-east, whom he eventually defeated in 1091. By 1095, he had succeeded in restoring the frontiers of the Empire in Europe to the Danube and the Adriatic. He then looked eastwards to Anatolia and the distant Euphrates. It was at this juncture that Alexius inadvertently precipitated a new and alarming crisis by appealing to the West for military aid. Unbeknownst to him, he had set in motion the avalanche of the Crusades.

The New Papacy

The second half of the 11th century was the heroic age of papal history. Reforming popes and their followers sought to purify the Church of what was seen as the taint of lay corruption, and to establish the superiority of spiritual power over the secular. Above all, this came to mean a struggle with the German emperors, who, from the 10th-century Ottonians onwards, considered themselves the heirs of Charlemagne.

The origins of papal reform

The intellectual position of the reforming papacy of the 11th century was essentially that set out by Leo the Great and Gelasius I in the 5th century: namely, that in all spiritual matters the pope superseded any king; however, at the turn of the first millennium, kings and emperors continued to treat bishoprics and abbeys as part of their royal domain. In the mid-11th century, four-fifths of the 140 monasteries attached to the monastery of Gorze in Lorraine were subject to a king. Little wonder: they were profitable and practical as instruments of government. The first great stand against this had been taken by Duke William "the Pious" of Aquitaine. In 910, he pronounced a curse on any layman who sought to interfere with Cluny Abbey, his vast new foundation in Burgundy. Over the next century and a half, this spirit of reform gained momentum, engendering both debate and pamphlet wars, as intellectuals and propagandists alike turned their thoughts to the dangers of purchasing clerical office (known as simony), the

wrongs of selling pardons and indulgences, and the political dimensions of religious orthodoxy. In 1048, the matter was still open: Pope Leo IX was nominated and invested with the ring and staff of his office by the German king Henry III. A year later, the same Leo stood before the relics of St Remigius at the Council of Rheims, where he asked in a deceptively innocent voice which of those bishops present had paid for their office. Most, including the Archbishop himself, had. Leo's reaction was so extreme that some bishops fled, some were censured, and the council was brought to a close with rigorous decrees. Christendom had received a shock from which it was not to recover.

Pope Gregory VII and King Henry IV

Leo died in 1054, Henry in 1056. While the papal court was filled with ardent reformers, the German throne was left to an infant, Henry IV, and for 20 years the papal star was in the ascendant. The most zealous of the reformers was Cardinal Humbert of Silva Candida, who in his *Book against Simoniacs* launched a coruscating attack on the entire relationship of seculars to the Church, in particular imperial investiture of bishops. Humbert objected profoundly to the fact that bishops were seen to receive their authority from laymen. His arguments found favour with Pope Alexander II (1061–73) and, most famously, Pope Gregory VII (1073–85). At this time, the principal weapon of the papacy was excommunication: total exclusion from Christian society and loss of all hope of salvation. Early in 1073, Alexander unleashed this weapon against five councillors of Henry IV who were seeking to influence the appointment of a new Archbishop of Milan. Alexander then died, leaving the new pope, Gregory, over-extended.

In 1076, a number of German bishops met at Worms and declared Gregory deposed, no doubt preferring the patronage of an emperor to the interference of a pope. Gregory responded in kind, excommunicating both the bishops and the emperor who had encouraged them. For those German

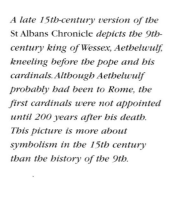

A late 15th-century version of the St Albans Chronicle *depicts the 9th-century king of Wessex, Aethelwulf, kneeling before the pope and his cardinals. Although Aethelwulf probably had been to Rome, the first cardinals were not appointed until 200 years after his death. This picture is more about symbolism in the 15th century than the history of the 9th.*

The Cleansing of the Temple

The greatest aim of the reforming papacy was to ensure that secular powers had no authority in Church matters. One of the justifications for the papacy's occasional militancy in enforcing this was Christ's cleansing of the Temple (depicted here by Giotto). Images of moneylenders and traders being driven out were used as shorthand for this belief by papalist patrons of art, particularly those like Gregory VII and Cardinal Humbert, who believed that simony was tantamount to selling the divine office. By their time, it had gained an added significance – the excesses of wealth and profits of banking among the elite of the Italian cities lay many snares for the faithful.

princes who resented Henry's rule, this was too good an opportunity to miss – if God's vicar did not support Henry, how could they? In the autumn of 1076, they sat in judgement on their emperor and declared that, if he had not received papal absolution by the following February, he would be deposed. Just in case he tried to seek this in person, they closed the passes through the Alps. Henry received his absolution at the eleventh hour, only after he had crossed the Alps on foot in secret and prostrated himself before the pope at Canossa, Italy, for four days. The humiliation was grave, but politically Henry emerged the winner.

Gregory died an exile from his beloved Rome, having been kidnapped by the very Norman forces he had hoped would protect him from political threats, but his voice is one of only a very few that echo down through the centuries. His struggles with Henry IV, often termed the investiture contest, were not simply about power, as his 11th- and 21st-century critics claim, but born of a world view in which the correct ordering of a divinely ordained Christian society was paramount. "Righteousness" was his constant refrain. He cursed those who "kept back their sword from blood, that is kept back their tongues from condemning wrong". As a "soldier of Christ", he revelled in military metaphors and mined deeply the Old Testament prophets, particularly Elijah and Jeremiah. His argument was not just that the spiritual should always take precedence over the secular whenever the two came into contact; it was also that the papacy itself lay at the heart of spiritual authority on earth. A saying of Leo the Great declared that, while other bishops have pastoral care attributed to them, the papacy alone has plenitude of power. If Gregory had adhered less closely to this precept, he might have found more support for his reforms elsewhere in the Church. But Gregory was never a politician; he was Christ's vicar and St Peter's heir.

The legacy of conflict

The papal reform movement is often given Gregory's name; however, when he died in 1085, it had a long history ahead of it, not least because of cogent imperial opposition. It was indeed true that Charlemagne had intervened in the affairs of the Church, sat in judgement on a pope, and dictated doctrinal issues. Henry IV never forgot that his father had deposed three popes and appointed three more.

The imperial crown, the symbol of the emperors' temporal power, was made deliberately high so that a cloth mitre, the symbol of ecclesiastical authority, could be worn underneath it. This same crown was worn by Emperor Frederick Barbarossa during his conflicts with Pope Alexander III a century later. At an ideological level (perhaps not always the level at which kings and popes thought), this crown stood at the crux of the issue: emperors believed that they, too, had a religious function, one that was ordained by God.

The most powerful imperial tract directed against Pope Gregory VII was called *On the Unity of the Church*; it argued that Gregory was disrupting God's order, and that the consequences of this disruption might be dire. This argument held good in political circles for much of the rest of the Middle Ages. In the mid-14th century, English kings were prohibited appeal to the papal court in any matter concerning English benefices. This statute, *Praemunire*, was to become one of Henry VIII of England's most powerful weapons in enforcing his split from Rome 150 years later.

The Bonds of Society

Traditional medieval wisdom divided society into three estates: the clergy, who prayed and looked to society's spiritual wellbeing; the warriors, who defended the land and people; and the labourers, whose toil supported the other two orders. Just as the reforming popes were concerned with the correct ordering of society on a European scale, so on a local scale each person had to perform his allotted duty.

A 14th-century Swiss illustration of the Dominican Eberhard of Sax praying before the altar of the Virgin Mary. The idea that the spiritual battles of monks were as important, if not more so, than the physical battles of soldiers grew in strength in the Middle Ages.

The ties that bound

In the 11th century, a few small independent proprietors still existed, but most arable land was exploited according to the manorial system. Generally speaking, a manor comprised a handful of neighbouring villages all dependent on and bound to a single lord's residence; its component fields were organized as a single agricultural endeavour. Peasants were granted smallholdings on an outlying portion of a manor in exchange for tending the inner core, the lord's demesne (lands). The servile nature of their tenure meant that they were legally unfree. They owed a heavy burden of agricultural services throughout the year, perhaps two or three days a week of ploughing, sowing, or carting, with additional duties at harvest. They might also owe more personal duties, which were often attached to specific tenancies within the manor, such as assisting on hunts, tending the lord's dogs, fencing game enclosures, or repairing the lord's hall. Duties were excused on holy days, and communities were always keen to venerate new saints; but for every saint's day the village priest was pressurized into

recognizing, a day of "voluntary" service was introduced by the lord.

There was some differentiation between classes of peasants according to how much land they held and what they owed, but most villages had no real economic hierarchy. Only the reeves – the supervisors of the manor – stood out. These men performed administrative functions on behalf of their lord and often did very well out of their positions. If a peasant did not render to his lord his due, it was the reeve and his bailiffs who came to exact it, and court records are full of accusations that reeves lined their own pockets in the process. Similar accusations were levelled occasionally at parish priests, who were entitled to a tithe – one-tenth – of all produce for the maintenance of the church and its offices. For all the attempts at reform by popes from Leo IX onwards, many parish priests took wives, bore weapons, and charged for the favours their position allowed like any layman.

Many minor crimes and some major ones were tried in the lord's manorial court. The records of one monastic court in the 13th century tell of men and

Medieval justice
Medieval kings and emperors prided themselves on their ability to dispense justice. Generally, punishments were fines and forfeits, or mutilation and execution. The most gruesome deaths were saved for traitors, counterfeiters, and, later, heretics. In much of Europe justice was private and seigneurial – nobles long defended their right to try and punish – but in Carolingian France and Anglo-Saxon England, justice was public. This image shows a trial and execution before the *witan*, representatives of the English shire.

A 15th-century French "calendar" illustrating 12 idealized scenes of labour corresponding roughly to the months of the agricultural year. Peasant obligations to sow, lamb, hunt, thresh, and even tread grapes for wine were the basis of medieval estate management.

women who were fined for petty theft, failing to turn up for jury service, illegal brewing, failing to ensure that they were members of a tithing (by which, in theory, unfree men in formerly Carolingian and Anglo-Saxon areas were associated in groups of 10 or 12 so that each would be responsible for the others' behaviour), and even allowing their cattle to trample the vicar's peas. Fines for evasion of labour dues were among the most common. Matters were even worse for peasants living in areas designated as forest land. Forest land was preserved for hunting, and French and English kings famously maintained huge tracts in which deer and boar were protected and encroachment was forbidden. Court records bear witness to the tensions forest law created among rural communities.

Changing priorities

Money was more important than labour to some lords, and on certain manors peasants held their land wholly or partially by rent. As the Middle Ages wore on and the labour pool grew as the population increased, this system became more and more common until often the demesne itself was let out. In addition to their rent, many peasants now provided their lord with a series of payments at births, deaths, and marriages, which marked their continued servile status. During the late 12th and 13th centuries, it became common for serfs, either individually or in groups, to buy their legal freedom for a lump sum, changing their status to that of rent-paying tenants. In theory, this should also have allowed them a greater degree of economic freedom; often, rent-paying tenants sought to bring areas of wasteland and woodland into profitable cultivation for themselves without their lord's knowledge. In practice, for many, this increased productivity did not necessarily counterbalance increased rent, and they were left with nothing but their labour to sell.

The single greatest stimulus to any regional economy was proximity to a growing, prosperous town, and urbanization and changes to the manorial system are closely linked. In northern Italy, the most urbanized part of medieval Europe, the old manors were breaking up, and leases replaced labour dues. By the late 12th century, the landlord was often not a noble at all, but a city-based merchant. By contrast, southern Italy was much less urbanized, and here the great manors endured, with most peasants remaining under the bonds of serfdom.

A similar pattern can be seen in the Low Countries. Around the recently developed industrial and commercial cities of Flanders, 12th-century peasants were gaining their freedom and pursuing their own goals, while in the more economically depressed areas of Namur and Luxembourg, most peasants remained serfs until the end of the Middle Ages. But the trend was not uniform: in places, the late 13th century saw a reaction to this by lords, who began to retrieve their labour services and take their lands back into direct cultivation. Many ecclesiastical estates had been reluctant to forego their services in the first place, as large communities of monks depended on the produce of their estates for their sustenance. Despite their periodic support for freeing serfs as a pious act, popes continued to legislate for the preserved integrity of ecclesiastical estates.

Knighthood

Towards the end of the 11th century, a new idea began to gain currency, the notion of the warrior as "the soldier of Christ". It came to focus on the ceremony in which a man was dubbed a knight. Here, in supposed opposition to the aristocratic violence that was almost endemic in northern Europe, the aspiring knight dedicated his sword to the altar and made a profession of vows to the service of the Church.

Ever since St Odo of Cluny wrote The Life of Gerald, *his pen-portrait of the perfect Christian knight, images in which Christ and his knights together vanquished evil were popular. Often, this was juxtaposed with images of tyrants in league with devils.*

A 15th-century French interpretation of The Romance of King Arthur and the Knights of the Round Table *by the 12th-century writer Chrétien de Troyes. By the later Middle Ages, "Arthurian" tournaments were a regular feature of noble life and a means of uniting martial combat with social display. Even the merchants of London were staging their own jousts by this time.*

The origins of knighthood

In the mid-12th century, the scholar Peter Abelard cautioned Abbess Héloïse against choosing a noble-born woman as prioress: "such a woman tends to be presumptuous and arrogant because of her birth". Although the word "noble" designated neither title nor office, there was something in the bloodline of certain families that meant that they and their contemporaries considered themselves such, and it was a quality that could not be bought or lost. Those seeking to include themselves in this class, and exclude others, compiled lengthy genealogies and controlled inheritance and marriages with paranoid care. The various medieval words for "knight", on the other hand, all have their origin in the profession of mounted warriors, with only occasional reference to descent. At the beginning of this period, some knights were simply employees of nobles, paid to do their fighting, while others were the younger sons of nobles and their cousins roving across the continent seeking to make a name for themselves. These young men often looked more like minor war bands than anything else, and medieval writers, especially churchmen, came to regard them as a public menace. A public-relations war developed.

In the 10th century, St Odo of Cluny had written of his ideal knight, Gerald of Aurillac, a man so pious that he fought only with the flat of his sword. Cluny was also behind the formation of certain principles that limited aristocratic violence to certain activities and certain times. In the 11th century, this idea was given its fullest expression by Popes Gregory VII and Urban II: knights, as soldiers of Christ, waged a war against the worldly agents of the Devil, just as monks fought their spiritual counterparts. In the 12th century, a further step was taken by the influential Cistercian abbot, Bernard of Clairvaux, who promoted an institutional form of religious knighthood by encouraging men to join the new military order of the Templars. Its members undertook both ordinary monastic vows and the defence of Jerusalem from the infidel. It was said that he preached his cause so persuasively that mothers locked up their sons for fear he would spirit them away.

Chivalry

The notion that there might be both heavenly and worldly honour in the profession of arms was an attractive one for young (and old) men seeking to assure or better their status. The nebulous collection of ideas that has developed around this notion is known as chivalry, from *chevalier*, the French word for knight. Books were written telling knights how to conduct themselves in every last regard, epics were composed to hold forth shining examples of excellence, and tournaments were fought to apply those examples to real life. Just how far chivalric ideals applied to reality is extremely uncertain. The chival-

ric epic poems known as *chansons de geste* ("songs of great deeds") show little interest in how noble actions impacted upon the rest of society, and, for all the prominence of the new literary notion of courtly love, noblewomen were still abducted and forced into marriages as often as they had ever been.

The German poet Gottfried von Strassburg engaged these double standards in his epic *Tristan*, written in the early 13th century. In his tale, the young Tristan studied literature, languages, music, wrestling, fencing, and hunting to become the perfect Arthurian knight, a physical and intellectual paradigm. After many adventures, he arrived at the court of King Mark, revealed as his uncle, who knighted him for his many past and anticipated virtues. Having woven his mythic tapestry so skilfully, however, Gottfried then tears it apart. Tristan lusts after the king's bride, Isolde, and together they deceive the king and plan the murder of the only witness to their crime. Tristan is forced into combat with Mark's champion, whom he strikes down in an orgy of gushing blood and shattered bone. Tristan, our hero, mocks the broken champion before hacking off his head. For Gottfried, often praised as a great chivalric writer, the reality of knighthood was all too evident.

Warfare

Perhaps the most vivid and extended descriptions of warfare in the Middle Ages are the various chronicles of the Crusades. Many were based on first-hand experience, and all have a common theme: hardship. One author describes the crusaders' march south from Acre, pursued by the Turks, shortly after the city fell in 1191: "Arrows and spears flew and hissed through the air. Even the brightness of the sun was darkened by the multitude of missiles, as though by the wintry density of hail or snow … The points of darts and arrows covered the ground so that if anyone wished to collect them, a single snatch would provide him with at least twenty."

Combat waged with blades, horses, and fire was always a horrifically bloody business, and wherever possible hunger and fear were the preferred weapons. An invading army needed to keep its supply lines open above all else, so would often besiege castles or towns that otherwise might attack its train of carts. In the 1050s, Duke William of Normandy, the future conqueror of England, sought to avoid open combat in northern France by mutilating prisoners as a means of persuading the citizens of recalcitrant towns to surrender. Despite this, the Normans were the most famous and feared knights in medieval Europe; their equipment and formations were recognized from England to Sicily, from Cordoba to Constantinople. Both are illustrated clearly in the depiction in the Bayeux Tapestry of the Battle of Hastings of 1066. The Normans fought on horseback – unlike the English, who fought on foot – and their cavalry employed a series of coordinated feints and outflanking manoeuvres. They wore heavy, knee-length mail coats, carried kite-shaped shields, and fought with sword, throwing spear, and couched lance (which went on to become the famous weapon of the joust). Perhaps most important of all, they developed a quick and ready base of operations, a timber tower on top of a huge earth mound within a fortified compound. These structures came to be known as motte and bailey castles; they were the tool by which much of England was subjugated.

In the early Middle Ages, the ports
of the Rhone delta had all carried
a considerable volume of trade. By
the end of the period, however,
natural silting had reduced all
but Marseilles to very minor
operations. Marseilles exercised a
corresponding influence, and, by
the 14th century, its merchants
were able to demand favourable
treatment in the Italian ports.

KINGDOMS AND COMMUNITIES

Medieval narrative sources often focus on kings and their nobles; lords and their peasants; popes and their priests. It is easy to think that social groups were always defined in terms of those above and those below. This is true in part, but it is potentially misleading. Membership of a village, town, province, guild, and, above all, kingdom were equally powerful, and in these ways community was at least as important as hierarchy.

The term "feudalism" is today used to refer to almost any oppressive or hierarchical system. When applied to the Middle Ages, the most common analogy is a pyramid: the king or emperor is at the very top with high-ranking nobles below him. They in turn are on top of a larger number of petty nobles and bureaucrats, all resting on a huge mass of impoverished peasants. Feudalism is sometimes used in the more specific sense of relations between nobles: one man might become the vassal of another by paying homage to him, swearing fidelity, and undertaking to provide him with soldiers if needed, in exchange for a piece of land (known as a "fief") and promises of good lordship. This constituted a feudal relationship and could only exist between freemen. Feudalism is sometimes extended to governmental systems: in Norman England, all land was held ultimately by the king, who granted it to his nobles on condition that they contribute a designated number of soldiers to the feudal host. These nobles might in turn grant a portion of their lands to their own men under a similar arrangement. It is easy to see how this concept can be used to explain the social structure of medieval Europe.

The reality was less clear cut, and there was a number of less formal relations into which men and women might enter. The words "vassal" and "fief" are less common in medieval documents than might be expected, and, even when they do appear, they probably conceal a variety of different relationships: ruler and subject; patron and client; landlord and tenant; employer and employee; general and soldier; bully and victim. How one stood in relation to one's peers was far more important than how one stood in relation to distant social inferiors or superiors. Concepts of nobility and freedom were not concrete. Among the most highly respected knights of the German kings were the *minisiteriales*. These skilled warriors and bureaucrats held considerable lands of the king, but they were not freemen in the eyes of the law. The case of the *ministeriales* is instructive. They formed part of a movement in which, as collective activity became more organized, bureaucracy developed. Literacy increased the range and power of propaganda, governments came to rely less on direct interpersonal relations, and feudal stereotypes become less applicable.

Law

In early medieval Europe, it was only kings who could legislate, but the bedrock of law throughout the West was unwritten custom. Even the "Roman law" in which parts of Italy took pride can be seen as not much more than another variety of custom. Customary law was enacted in formally constituted courts. Regular occasions of collective judgement did much to foster not only a sense of community, but also a readiness and ability on the part of those communities to act on their own account. During the 12th and 13th centuries, the strengthening of government began to transform law by emphasizing one source of its authority and enforcement above all others. More and more crimes came to incur formal penalties, but responsibility for the maintenance of law and order depended throughout on collective self-policing. It is a fact of medieval European state-building that the more central authority was enforced, the more the foundations upon which it rested were strengthened.

Nation-States

An individual's horizons might close around a small village or extend beyond Christendom, but medieval writers almost always thought of the kingdom as the highest of all secular communities. Some kingdoms, such as those of northern Spain, appeared less united than some smaller units of government, such as Brittany, but throughout the Middle Ages kingdoms were normally perceived as the ideal type of political unit.

The community of the realm

A kingdom was more than the geographical area within which a king ruled. Just as the Church, although united in universal faith, varied its customs according to local tradition, so a kingdom comprised and was to be identified with a "people", a natural and inherited community of tradition and descent. From at least the 10th century, writers combined biblical and classical elements to concoct myths of the origin and descent of their peoples. From the 12th century these myths were copied in vernacular poems and stories intended for popular audiences. By the 13th they were even creeping into political documents. But common descent and law alone did not make a kingdom. One of the most important political developments of this period was that in many areas the loyalties of kingship formulated in the first millennium after Rome came to coincide with solidarities of supposed common descent and law. In part, this was due to the increasing role of representation and consultation in medieval

government. It would be wrong to view medieval councils and parliaments as striving towards modern representative government: direct election was almost unknown in the Middle Ages, but the idea that the leading men of a community might represent it to its king, and vice versa, was perfectly natural. The development of a nexus that bound local communities into the community of the realm was fundamental to the building of medieval states.

England

The expression "community of the realm" is particularly associated with England. The various English kingdoms were not united under a single king until the late 9th century, but they had long shared a common identity as a single people with a single name, language, and Church. It was an accommodating identity: in the 10th century, there was a clear distinction drawn between Danish invaders on the one hand and Englishmen and women who happened to be of Danish descent on the other. The

By the end of the 12th century, England and France had long disputed lands in Normandy, Anjou, and Aquitaine. Richard the Lionheart of England built the imposing Château Gaillard at Les Andeleys as a bridgehead into Normandy, which his brother, John, had recently ceded to the French. It fell in 1204.

The Hundred Years War

For the greater part of the period 1338–1453, England and France were formally at war. Since the 19th century, historians have called this time of trouble the Hundred Years War. The name is misleading. Famous campaigns such as Poitiers (1356) and Agincourt (1415) were separated by long periods, sometimes decades, of inactivity. The crux of the issue was England's claim to parts of northern and central France, at times even the throne. In theory, France should have proved the stronger, but English naval power protected the island from all but France's allies in the north, the Scots, who often proved England's most dangerous and immediate foe. By the mid-15th century, England had ceded almost all of its possessions in France, but neither country really emerged the winner. Each had had their bureaucratic fiscal machinery placed on a war footing, each had had their national identities forcibly reassessed, and each had lost many lives and much money for little tangible political gain.

Norman Conquest of 1066 did not create a new kingdom, and, by the 12th century, Anglo-Norman historians were lauding the patriotic principles enjoyed by "we English". William the Conqueror occupied the English throne for 21 years; he owed much of his ongoing success to the fact that, although a foreigner, he sat at the hub of a sophisticated governmental system that frustrated anything other than very localized resistance.

The following century saw prolonged civil war, and much of this cohesion was lost. In large part it was regained by the demands that late 12th-century kings made for men and money in order to fight their wars in France. Conflict with the French kings over Normandy and other northern French lands was the single greatest legacy of the Norman Conquest. Opposition to these demands was in itself a powerful unifying force. In the 13th century, the expression "community of the realm" was invoked against excessive royal demands, but royal government did not foster unity simply by its oppression. The 12th-century extension of royal justice sent judges on regular circuits of the country, administering increasingly uniform procedures. When there were complaints, they were about corruption, not about the principle of royal control. It is significant that, when King John was brought to task by rebel barons in 1215, it was not less royal justice that they wanted, but more.

France

In the early 10th century, the division of the Frankish kingdom into two halves was still very recent, and, although both were occasionally called the kingdom of the Franks, it is unlikely that either had very much regnal solidarity. When Hugh Capet, the founder of the line of Capetian kings, made himself king in 987, most of his kingdom took little notice of him. But the Capetians had remarkable staying power, if only because they were very fortunate in producing male heirs at the right times, and confined their political objectives to the area immediately around Paris. Beyond that, French nobles were able to administer their territories as princes and occupy their castles with impunity. It is telling that Abbot Suger of St Denis thought that the co-operation of French nobles against the German emperor's invasion of 1124 was unusual enough to be Francia's finest hour.

Wars with England over Normandy did as much to strengthen national solidarity in France as they did across the Channel. The reconquest of English-held Normandy and Anjou by the French king Philip II, most notably at the Battle of Bovines, which frustrated King John of England's claims in France, followed closely by the French-led Albigensian crusade against the Cathar heretics in the south of the country, transformed the position of the early 13th-century French monarchy. It is no coincidence that references to the Trojan descent of the Franks first appear at this time. Initially at least, notions of the French kingdom faltered on the language barrier of *oïl* and *oc*, and sometimes "Francia" was taken to apply only to the north. Nonetheless, contemporaries were coming to think in terms of a common law that applied to the entire kingdom and of the king as having ultimate jurisdiction over it.

Towns and Communes

The growth of towns reflects the curve of medieval economic history, but it also heralded the rediscovery of a lost way of living. At a time when much of the rural population was bound to the soil by servile obligations, the townsman was free to move about as he wished, change occupation, and even take orders in the Church without the approval of any lord. This freedom fostered greater political ambitions.

The Italian city-states

Cities had been important in Roman Italy, but their administrative and cultural identities were shattered by the Lombardic invasions of the 6th century. Three hundred years later, the Carolingians still had no effective control of this part of their empire, and local counts were able to do more or less as they wished. The Ottonian emperors sought to use bishops (whose appointment they could manipulate) as a means of exerting influence, but the picture remained confused. Meanwhile, opportunities offered by the expansion of the Mediterranean economy reinvigorated certain north Italian towns as trade centres and encouraged the growth of a middle class. In these uncertain times, members of the old comitial families and new merchants formed sworn associations in large cities and small communities alike, seeking to establish their power – sometimes in conflict with the bishop, sometimes in alliance. These associations often made claims to be representatives of the "people" in an appeal to historic precedent, but they were never public bodies in origin.

The struggles with the reforming popes did much to shake imperial rule in northern Italy from the late 11th century onwards. Emperors soon granted concessions to the leading men of certain cities in exchange for their nominal support. The development of town consulates (connected to the Roman institution of the same name by nostalgia alone) followed soon after. To balance the claims of rival civic factions that often erupted into street fights, many cities appointed professional administrators from outside their walls to serve as head, or *podesta*, for a fixed term, on condition that they abstain from all trade and commerce.

Each city had its own army and often navy that fought other cities for commercial advantage: to capture a rival city's standard was a great triumph. The accession of Frederick Barbarossa in 1152, however, saw in an emperor determined to regain his traditional rights, and began a century of political struggle in which old differences between the city-states were temporarily set aside. In 1167, the towns of Lombardy formed the Lombard League, renewing their alliance in 1226 on the accession of the ambitious Frederick II. The cities of Tuscany were slower to organize themselves, but they, too, formed an alliance in 1198. Barbarossa was defeated roundly by the Lombard cities at Legnano in 1176. In the treaty of the Peace of Constance of 1183, he accepted the right of the cities to elect their own consuls, build fortifications, and govern their hinterlands.

Venice

Venice was unlike all other Italian city-states. The earliest settlements around its lagoons had been dependent on Byzantium; however, in the Middle Ages, Venetians cultivated the idea that their city had always been an independent republic under the patronage of St Mark. At its head was the

A page of the 15th-century Guild Book of the Barber Surgeons of York. *Guilds were a common feature of medieval urban life. Sworn fraternities of trade or craft, they managed their affairs and protected their members in similar ways to modern unions and golf clubs. Unlike lofty physicians or lowly apothecaries, the barber surgeons cut hair, knocked out teeth, and amputated fingers.*

doge, elected by the General Assembly, which comprised representatives of a relatively small number of leading families, some of which claimed Roman descent. Despite occasional accusations of nepotism, culminating in the assassination of Doge Vital II in 1172, this system appears to have been far more stable than that of *podesta* practised elsewhere: although only 150 families were implicated in rule in a population of 120,000, Venice was relatively untroubled by faction. It had no hinterland to speak of and so was entirely dependent on sea trade and its colonies, both of which were hugely boosted by the Crusades. Venetians wangled preferential trading rights in Constantinople, tenders to transport Crusaders to the Holy Land, and lending contracts to bankroll the whole enterprise. To all intents and purposes, they engineered the Fourth Crusade of 1204.

Northern European towns

Canterbury, the first and most important cathedral town of England, could claim no more continuity with its Roman origins than the towns of northern Italy; however, by the 9th century its inhabitants were calling themselves "portmen" from the Latin *portus*, meaning trading place. Archaeological finds in German towns suggest that they, too, were on the rise economically, long before town identity began to develop a political aspect in the 11th and 12th centuries. Market law is referred to in both France and Germany in the 11th century, and if grants of rights to hold markets and gather tolls were more common for the towns of Germany and Flanders than France, that was probably because royal authority in France was too weak to make royal charters worth having. The tolls townsmen paid or from which they were exempt consolidated their common interests. Common funds are suggested by the fact that at least two English towns had paid a lump sum for their local mint by 1086.

The late 11th and 12th centuries saw many old northern towns acquire a more complete independence, often by fairly unsystematic means. In 1070, the citizens of Le Mans cast off the control of their bishop and proclaimed themselves to be a commune. Worms, Cologne, and other Rhineland cities soon followed suit. In the ensuing two centuries of conflict, the cities generally held their own against the bishops, largely because of the support of the German emperors, who found the new communes to be powerful allies against the Church. Most of the larger German towns came to be designated "imperial cities", dependent only on the emperor.

As imperial power diminished over the period, so the cities' autonomy increased, and in time many banded together as leagues against those princes who still sought to exert their authority upon them.

Certain Swiss cities (then under German imperial rule), including Zug, Zurich, and Bern, entered the Swiss confederation as individual cantons. As in Italy, the apparent absence of a closed governing class in the towns of northern Europe does not mean that there were no discontents; however, the rulers of these towns were more closely supervised from outside than were those in Italy, so serious conflicts do not seem to have come to a head so quickly. When they did, they were often expressed through craft associations. The cloth city of Flanders saw the most fierce conflicts of economic interest, because the range and complexity of the cloth trade made it easier for its wealthier merchants to abuse their position by excluding weavers and fullers from the town franchise.

In France and England, the communal movement never really gained momentum, despite the best efforts of London. In both countries, relations between the crown and the cities remained largely good, however, not least because the new commerical classes of the cities provided the crown with a useful ally against the nobility. In the 13th century, English cities became integrated into a system of parliamentary representation.

At various times, more than 200 cities belonged to the Hanseatic League, a far-flung confederation of "free cities of the sea" stretching from the Atlantic to the Gulf of Finland. The English word "sterling" derives from "Easterling", an epithet commonly applied to Hansa merchants.

Magna Carta

In 1215, rebel English barons, tired of what they perceived to be autocratic and incompetent rule, forced King John to sign a great charter of rights and liberties. Although tentative steps had been taken elsewhere, England became the first country in Europe to have a written constitutional check on the king's power. It was to become one of the most famous documents in the English-speaking world.

The royal seal of Henry II of England. The royal seal was often attached to documents issued by the chancery. It served both as a readily identifiable means of authentication and a powerful and widely circulated image of the king in majesty, enthroned and crowned with orb and sword.

Orford Castle, Norfolk, England was built by Henry II between 1165 and 1173 as a check on the Earl of Norfolk. It cost more than £1400 to erect. The design is unusual in that it is cylindrical inside and polygonal outside, with three projecting towers.

The background to Magna Carta

By the 13th century, England had a long history of participatory government. Anglo-Saxon kings consulted local representatives on many matters and wrote to their subjects promising good lordship. In 1100, Henry I, youngest son of William the Conqueror, issued his celebrated Coronation Charter, in which he promised a more settled and less savage regime than that of his predecessor and brother, William Rufus. Addressed to the entire country, it was intended to win back the much-needed support of alienated barons. The tide, however, was against reconciliation. In the following century, expanding royal government saw the rise of non-noble officials, the overburdening of already cumbersome judicial procedure, and increasing disregard for the property rights and dignities of the aristocracy. The murder of Thomas à Becket under Henry II in 1170 provided a further pretext for dissent. The situation became

more tense in the first decade of the 13th century when King John lost a succession of disputed lands in northern France to the French king, Philip Augustus. Henry's Coronation Charter became a rallying point for disaffected nobles and churchmen. In 1206, a dispute arose over King John's unwillingness to appoint as Archbishop of Canterbury Stephen Langton, a leading intellectual light and the pope's preferred candidate, providing the excuse for open rebellion. A tentative peace was reached in 1213, but the situation remained hostile. Faced with military threat and the combined weight of his barons and bishops, John was forced to set his seal to the rebel barons' demands enshrined in the Magna Carta,. on 15 June 1215. To add insult to injury, Langton officiated over the proceedings.

The clauses

Although the Magna Carta contains at least one shining expression of principle – "no freeman shall be arrested, imprisoned, dispossessed, outlawed, exiled, or in any way ruined except by judgement of his peers or by the law of the land" (clause 39) – most of its more than 60 clauses are concerned with administrative or legal details. Some were aimed at dismantling John's machinery of control: the expulsion of foreign mercenaries; the remission of huge fines; and the dismissal of certain named royal officials. Others attacked certain economic restrictions: fish weirs were to be removed from specified rivers; foreign merchants were to be treated reasonably in all things; and all restrictions relating to royal forest law were to be lifted. One clause, heavy with future significance, stated that the taxes known as "scutage" and "aid" would not be levied without "the common counsel of the kingdom". In an odd paradox, the rebels did not want less royal justice, but more, and the law of the land was trumpeted in opposition to the king's mere will. Many of the clauses sought to make the machinery of justice more regular, equitable, and accessible. The most remarkable innovation came in clause 61. This established a committee of 25 barons

The murder of Thomas à Becket

Thomas à Becket was Chancellor of England (1155–62), then Archbishop of Canterbury (1162–70) under Henry II. Although initially a staunch supporter of the king, he became increasingly interested in the cause of the established Church and so became a thorn in Henry's side. In 1170, a small group of knights broke into Canterbury Cathedral and murdered Thomas on the altar, perhaps acting on the king's instructions. European public opinion was such that the next year the king appeared in sackcloth and ashes before the cathedral clergy. Thomas was quickly venerated as a saint, and images of his martyrdom proliferated across Europe.

before whom any complaints of infringements by the king were to be brought. If these barons judged that the king had not made good within 40 days, the 25 were permitted to seize his castles, lands, and other royal properties until such time as he did so. A general oath was sworn stating that the 25 were to be supported by "the commune of the whole land".

Magna Carta's legacy

The charter is renowned throughout the English-speaking world; however, this fame is due more to the use made of it by 17th-century English parliamentarians in their struggles with the Stuart kings, and the subsequent export of this newly fostered myth to New England, than to its intrinsic merits. At the end of 1215, it was a failure. Magna Carta was intended to bring peace, but instead provoked war. It was legally valid for no more than three months, during which time it was never properly executed. However, between the death of King John in 1216 and the majority of his son and heir, Henry III, in 1225, it was reissued three times with minor and major revisions. The fourth and final version was eventually confirmed in Parliament. Three of its clauses still stand on the English Statute Book, and others have only recently departed (the clause referring to fish weirs was only removed in 1970). The animating principles of consent to taxation, due process, and the rule of law are all present in Magna Carta.

Magna Carta was intimately connected with developing political theories in the 12th century – in his *Policraticus*, the scholar John of Salisbury had written of the justification of tyrannicide – and these theories bore some relation to reality. In 1183, Frederick Barbarossa had conceded practical independence of imperial rule to the Lombard cities. In 1188, King Alfonso IX of Léon promulgated ordinances conferring important privileges on his nobles. In 1205, King Peter II of Aragon drew up similar ordinances for his subjects in Catalonia, although they were never enacted. King Andrew II of Hungary granted his subjects a collection of rights under the Golden Bull of 1222. The English charter was part, albeit the most detailed example, of a Europe-wide movement towards a recognition of the constitutional rights of the community of the realm. Of course, there were problems. Just as the American Declaration of Independence ignored slaves, so, too, Magna Carta made no mention of the unfree, and in effect the "judgement by peers" was intended to ensure that barons looked after their own. But even though Magna Carta was only an active piece of legislation during the ten years of Henry III's minority, it has lived on as a powerful myth for centuries.

Trade, Industry, and Agriculture

In much of Western Europe, the most important economic developments that took place before the modern industrial revolution were during the High Middle Ages. Beginning in the 10th century in some parts of Europe, an economic boom lasted until the first decades of the 14th century.

Although the Middle Ages saw a great commercial expansion, many people maintained an ambiguous or even wholly damning view of money and its temptations. This early engraving depicts a three-horned devil with tail and goat's legs pouring money into the fire.

Trade

By the end of the first millennium, steady population growth had encouraged the exploitation of new land, the increase of food production, and improvements in communications; much energy was devoted to draining marshland, clearing forests, and building bridges, roads, and docks. These developments, together with the ending of the Viking and Magyar threats, created conditions in which merchants with contacts in the East (and there had always been some willing to take their chances throughout even the most dangerous periods) could do very well for themselves. Ships docked initially in Venice, Amalfi, Pisa, and Genoa laden with silks and spices from Byzantium and the Muslim empires, and returned eastward weighed down with timber, iron, and cloth.

The Crusades provided a great impetus to expansion in the south, and, by the 14th century, the Mediterranean cities were trading in almost any commodity from figs to firs, indigo to ivory. There was an ever more lucrative east–west trade in slaves (it betrays a grim truth that the word has a common origin with Slav). The growth of the Mongol empire in the 13th century offered yet more opportunities in the Far East, first exploited by Venetian merchants and, in particular, a certain family called Polo: their travels from 1271–92 are famously recorded by the younger son, Marco. Even bolder were the Vivaldi brothers of Genoa, who, 200 years before Columbus, set out to find the Indies via a westerly route. They never returned.

Trade in the north of Europe did not have the same level of risk as Italian trade. It was less dominated by high-value, low-volume goods, less was invested in each individual shipment, and so correspondingly the whole business was less precarious. Bremen, Hamburg, Elbe, and Lübeck were the northern counterparts of the four main Italian centres of trade. Associations of merchants known as *hansas* handled grain, fish, timber, metals, salt, honey, firs, and the other raw materials of the north. They formed a powerful economic mesh incorporating England, the Low Countries, Poland, Russia, Hungary, and Scandinavia, with northern Germany at the centre.

Industry

Growth was not confined to the Mediterranean and Baltic. The Low Countries saw great economic expansion, much of which was centred on Bruges. The city owed its prominence to cloth; after agriculture, textile manufacture was the single greatest industry of the Middle Ages. Flemish commercial links with England and Germany were established in the early 9th century and held fast up to the end of the 13th century. Early successes owed much to the ready availability of raw materials such as wool, hemp, dyes, flax, teasels, and fullers' earth (used as a detergent), together with a growing urban workforce. As the industry expanded, imports of wool from England and Spain, exotic dyes from the East, and alum (mineral salts used for cleansing cloth and fixing dyes) played an ever greater part. The great Flemish merchants of the first half of this period maintained a stranglehold on the cities' weavers and fullers to generate vast profits; however, by the later 13th century a series of urban revolts had rocked the merchant associations, and the industry entered a steady decline. By the early 14th century, rivals in England, Italy, and Aragon had taken over much of their business.

Most 18th-century industries were already developed in the 13th century: coal was mined, metal ores extracted, iron smelted, silk spun, and leather worked. With these pursuits came increasing mechanization, of which the best example is the mill. Water mills of various descriptions had been common across medieval Europe from at least the late 11th century. *The Domesday Book* (1086) lists more than 5000 in England, and by the late 12th century few rural communities would have been without one. Windmills soon followed, and, in the 13th century, the development of the water-powered fulling mill (which thickened and felted cloth) dragged much

The development of money

In the course of the Middle Ages, money increasingly became the favoured means of exchange. It had the obvious advantages over barter and goods in that it was portable and measurable, but that does not mean it was accepted everywhere – merchants sometimes preferred spices. Nonetheless, more and more peasants paid their taxes in coins, and such was the success of the small currency that the number of grams of silver to the pound-tale (i.e. 240 pennies) in France fell from 80 to 22 between 1250 and 1500. Gold was particularly associated with the great trading and banking centres of Italy. This Genoese coin also makes a political point – it was minted by the imperialist Ghibeline party.

industry out of the towns and into the countryside. There the mills worked wool, ground corn, tanned leather, beat metal, and even made paper, first manufactured in Fabriano at the end of the 13th century.

Agriculture

Much of medieval Europe enjoyed highly specialized farming arrangements best illustrated by the wide variety of wines available. Throughout the Middle Ages, however, cereal production was the basis of farming; even animal husbandry played little part in most lives. Wheat and rye were sown in the autumn and reaped between June and August. The medieval varieties did not grow well on poor soil and succumbed quickly to harsh winters, but their grains could easily be threshed free of their husks and ground to a fine flour which could be baked into bread. Oats and barley cropped rather better on poorer soils and because sown in the spring were less subject to bad weather. These grains produced only a low-grade flour that would not rise, so most oats were served as a porridge or fed to animals, while barley was malted to produce beer, the staple drink of medieval Europe.

For the most part, these crops were combined in a three-field rotational system comprising an autumn-sown crop, a spring-sown crop, and a fallow. Despite this system, most soil was over-used and under-manured, and so yields declined over the years. Improvements in ploughing techniques after the introduction of asymmetrical metal shares helped, and the incorporation of legumes into the system, especially peas and beans, not only benefited the medieval diet, but also reintroduced nitrogen into the depleted soil. Nonetheless, there was little concerted effort to improve soil fertility, and the growing population was provided for mostly by bringing new land into cultivation.

Most trade in the Indian Ocean was in high-value, low-volume goods; these boats are laden with bales and barrels, probably containing spices and oils. This was one of the reasons why a safe westerly route was so important: loss of a single ship could mean economic ruin for a merchant.

The Black Death

The Black Death was the most devastating epidemic to strike Europe. Many contemporaries viewed it as a sign that the end of the world was nigh; many modern historians as the end of an era. Cathedrals begun before its onset remained unfinished into modern times, while the great quadrangles of Oxford University exist only because the city beneath them was laid waste by the plague. The economic consequences of the Black Death are sometimes difficult to see, but its social and emotional consequences for the people of Europe are all too clear.

Medieval churches and churchyards were full of grisly images of Death personified. From the middle of the 14th century, plague was a familiar feature of the European experience and representations of Death as king became more and more common. This one comes from a 15th-century French book of hours by René d'Anjou, King of Sicily.

One of the more ghoulish side effects of the Black Death of 1348-9 was the increasing popularity of the danse macabre, *or dance of death, and illustrations of it. This anonymous engraving calls to mind the effigies of cadavers often featured on later medieval tombs beneath a truer effigy of the deceased.*

The onset

The Black Death was brought to Europe from Asia. In the mid-1340s, a group of Tartar warriors on campaign in China became infected. By 1346, they had brought the disease to their home in the Crimea, where it killed around 100,000 people. In the resulting pandemonium, Christian merchants, an unpopular minority, were made scapegoats for this apocalyptic horror, and, towards the end of the year, the Genoese trading outpost Caffa, now Feodosia on the Crimean coast, was besieged by a Tartar army. The army quickly succumbed to the plague, but as a parting shot catapulted infected corpses over the Italians' walls. As soon as the siege was lifted, the Genoese merchants fled the city, but they were not nearly quick enough to escape contagion; the disease appeared wherever their galleys touched shore. Sicily, Calabria, and the port cities of Genoa and Marseilles were all infected by the end of 1347. By the end of 1348, the plague had spread across much of Western Europe. By 1349, it had reached most of Germany and the British Isles and even made inroads into Scandinavia. By 1351, it was all but gone, although sporadic outbreaks blighted the remainder of the Middle Ages.

The Black Death was an inexplicable horror; it did not even receive its name until the 17th century. Today we know it to have been a deadly cocktail of three diseases. The primary component was bubonic plague, a disease carried in the blood of infected rats and spread by fleas, which causes its victims to break out in great tumours or buboes. It kills more than two-thirds of those infected in less than a week. It combined with pneumonic plague, an altogether more virulent disease that attacks the lungs. Spread by coughing, it is lethal in under two days. The third and rarest component was septicaemic plague, a disease that swamps the bloodstream with bacilli in less than two hours; it kills long before buboes have time to appear.

Population

Population in medieval Europe is very difficult to estimate because the necessary records do not exist. It may have peaked at the very beginning of the 14th century, then in places begun a gradual decline. What is certain is that the Black Death caused a massive dislocation. The parish register of Givry, in Burgundy, survives to tell a grim tale. Before the onset of the plague, it recorded an average of almost 40 deaths a year, suggesting a population of about one thousand. In 1348, the death toll jumped to 649, of which 630 occurred between July and November. This horrific record is far from exceptional; it is mirrored in such records as there are for taxation, burials, and census. Infants accounted for a high proportion of deaths, and each outbreak must have led to several generations of diminished birth rate until its effects had been exhausted. Each locality suffered its own individual fate – some escaped entirely – and generalizations are almost impossible; however, at least one-fifth of Europe's population died in 1348-9.

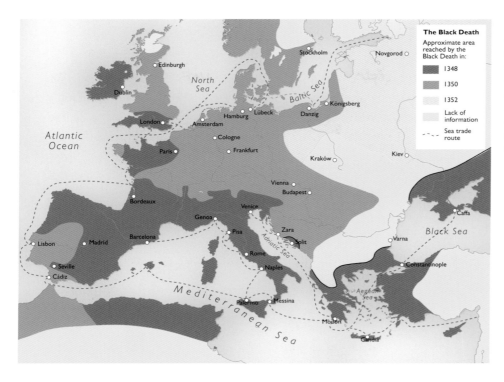

The Black Death spread across Europe with alarming speed. Broadly, coastal areas were affected earlier than inland areas, and those coastal areas that were hit first were connected to each other by sea trade routes. It is easy to see how so few ships could spread the plague across the continent.

Economic consequences

Fields went unploughed and crops unharvested. Immediate shortages led to panic buying, and prices rose. Many better-off families fled cities where infection appeared to be worse. (In 1351, Boccaccio wrote *The Decameron,* the story of ten noblemen and women who fled the plague in Florence and whiled away their time in telling tales; although fiction, it mirrors reality.) But these were all short-term consequences. Within three or four years, they had passed, and Europe was left to face more serious consequences.

In the first decade of the 14th century when population was at its peak, good agricultural land was scarce, and much marginal land was brought into cultivation. Peasant labour, meanwhile, was abundant, and so land values were high and wages were low. The Black Death reversed this relationship. The reduction of the labour force by at least one-fifth made it a relatively scarce commodity. Whereas once manorial courts had been inundated with peasants bidding against each other for land, surviving peasants were now able to dictate their own terms. Landlords resisted and attempted to reimpose servile obligations, leading to a bitter and often successful peasant backlash across Europe, of which the best-known examples are the French peasant uprising of 1357 (the Jacquerie) and the English Peasants Revolt in 1381. At the same time, total demand for produce was reduced, and so village communities could focus their attentions on farming better soils. Survivors and the subsequent generations enjoyed a better quality of life.

Social consequences

More land could never make up for the loss of loved ones. For medieval writers, the plague was a cataclysm; as one English monk described it, "it is uncertain whether any of Adam's race will survive to tell this tale". Images of death and decaying corpses began to feature more prominently in painting, literature, and sculpture, and the morbid dance of death became a regular feature of village life.

In Germany, notions that the plague was a form of divine retribution for man's sinfulness gave rise to two peculiar and unpleasant phenomena. The Brotherhood of Flagellants had their origin in the more or less widely accepted belief that mortification of the flesh might assist the remission of sins. Highly organized and, initially, very well respected bands of men and women travelled from town to town, beating themselves viciously in public ceremonies of expiation. Others directed their anger and fear outwards. Between 1348 and 1351, thousands of Jews were massacred in organized pogroms across Germany and in the neighbouring countries. Like the Christians at Coffa, they were seen as outsiders whose "perversions" had brought down this dreadful punishment and whose blood might buy salvation.

For many members of the upper ranks of society, hunting was the focus of their cultural and social life. Often their tenants were required to turn out to act as beaters for the hunt.

CULTURAL LIFE

Thinkers of the Renaissance looked back on this period as "a middle age" in which nothing of importance was achieved. The term has stuck, but looking back we can see a constant flow of artistic and intellectual creativity running throughout history. Cathedrals and illuminated manuscripts seize the imagination because the lost timber-framed houses and unrecorded songs cannot. Magnificent though it is, our view of medieval cultural life could in fact be a very distorted one.

The difficulties of understanding medieval culture are best appreciated through its music. Secular music was rarely given written notation before the 13th century, nor were its lyrics set down in ink. The English *"Sumer is icumen in"* ("Summer has come") is a rare exception, but we can have no idea of whether or not it is a typical composition of its time. Certainly it must have been one among an innumerable many. Manuscript illustrations depict musicians at every turn plucking harps, bowing viols, strumming gitterns (a guitar-like instrument), hammering dulcimers, and blowing bagpipes. Nor was all of this necessarily "low culture". For example, the minstrels on campaign with Henry V at Agincourt were paid 12 pence a day, twice what an archer earned and as much as a master surgeon. Certain medieval theorists even believed that music and medicine were mutually complimentary.

Music was part of the curriculum of medieval scholastic study and was inextricably bound up with the Church, so it inevitably became the subject of theological and intellectual debate. The greatest legacy of medieval church music is the wholly choral plainchant and polyphony of the daily services, but at the time it was a hotly debated issue. What was an appropriate degree of ornamentation for divine worship? At what point did a monk begin to take more pleasure in the music than in his worship of God? How might music best reflect the wonder of creation? These types of question make it tempting to view music-making as an academic exercise. Was function ultimately more important than aesthetics in church music? It only takes a sympathetic ear a moment to decide

that this was not the case, but these are the types of difficulty that thinkers and artists of the Middle Ages sought to overcome. The struggle is an unfamiliar one to us, and, while we might agree to take medieval culture on its own terms, identifying the terms themselves is not always easy.

What is certain about music in the Middle Ages is its universality. Similarly, grand architecture would have touched the lives of many – when the monasteries were torn down during the Reformation, it left ugly scars on the psyches of many small 16th-century communities.

Literature, however, remained far more selective throughout the Middle Ages. The interests of most medieval literary works were either courtly or ecclesiastical, and many were composed for a particular wealthy patron, although they may have had a wider audience through performance. That is not to say that the population of medieval Europe was largely illiterate. Many commercial activities required a relatively high degree of practical literacy and numeracy, and from at least the 13th century, manuals were written for almost every small business imaginable. In the urban schools of Italy, at the forefront of commerce, writing, calculation, and vernacular languages were taught to the exclusion of the classics. In Florence in 1338, out of a population of about 90,000, approximately 10,000 children were being taught the rudiments of reading and writing. In England, it is estimated that 30 per cent of the 15th-century population could read. These statistics compare favourably with literacy levels in Europe during the Industrial Revolution.

Education and Learning

Most Christian scholarship at the beginning of this period was rooted deeply in the work of the pagan philosophers, Aristotle and Plato, as preserved and interpreted by the Church Fathers and scholars of the late Roman Empire. But the early 12th century saw reason applied to many old problems with new vigour, heralding an intellectual revolution.

Well-known masters were able to attract students from across Europe. This representation, one of many, comes from a 14th-century manuscript of the Great Chronicles of France.

The Middle Ages, in particular the 14th century, saw a proliferation of places of learning, many with reputations for certain specializations. The finest Roman lawyers sought Bologna, the finest canon lawyers Paris. There was a good deal of cross-fertilization between the different types of institution. The oldest universities generally have their origins in the private schools of well-known teachers, who might themselves have been taught in a cathedral or monastery.

Scholastic humanism

In the 11th and 12th centuries, most learning and intellectual debate took place in cathedral schools such as the one presided over by St Bernard at Chartres. Students studied and masters debated the seven liberal arts of antiquity – the quadrivium of arithmetic, geometry, astronomy, and musical theory, and the *trivium* of logic, grammar, and rhetoric. It had long been held that the sciences of the ancient pagan world had their proper place in a Christian curriculum, as they played a part in the huge task of interpreting the Bible (albeit in ways that may seem odd or forced to us today); however, scholarship had vested little confidence in the potential of human beings. From the late 11th century, however, scholars such as Bernard of Clairvaux, Guibert of Nogent, and Peter Abelard turned their attention to the problems of the inner self. The 12th century saw an influx of hitherto unknown pagan works of science and philosophy from Byzantium and the Muslim East, most importantly new contributions from Aristotle,

which demanded a rethinking of the relationship between the laws which governed the material and the spiritual worlds. By the mid-12th century, a new, vibrant tradition of thought had gained momentum – scholastic humanism. This early humanism had nothing to do with the materialist humanism of the Renaissance three centuries later. Instead, it involved a deep intellectual concern with the role of people as individuals within an ordered universe, created by a God who himself became flesh so that he might experience and redeem the human condition. It became the driving force behind the century's intellectual, artistic, and literary endeavours.

Peter Abelard

Peter Abelard's fame today is due largely to a long autobiographical letter in which he laments his treatment at the hands of orthodox scholars and recounts his rather seedy love affair with a young noblewoman, Héloïse, as a result of which he was mutilated by her relatives and retired into a monastery in disgrace. But his fame in the early 12th century as a maverick teacher and writer of firecracker theology did much to establish Paris, where he was based, as the wellspring of intellectual renaissance. As a young man, he renounced the military career that his father had planned for him and travelled from cathedral to cathedral first to learn from then to debate publicly with some of the most renowned theologians of the time. By his own account, he bested them all and struck out on his own. His *Treatise on the Unity and Trinity of God* of 1121 turned this sparring into official Church condemnation. The work engaged the nature of universals, or what was truly real at a philosophical level, which had provoked debate between the contemporary Realist (Platonic) and Nominalist (Aristotelian) schools. Plato believed that only ideal forms were truly real, whereas Aristotle held that only individual things were fully real. Abelard sought to reconcile the two, but many Church officials considered the work overly dependent on pagan thought, and it was publicly burned. In another work, *Sic et Non* (literally, *Yes and No*), Abelard set

Intellectual and Religious Centres of Learning

- Universities evolving from pre-13th century schools
- Universities founded in the 13th century
- Universities founded in the 14th century
- Cathedral school
- Monastery school

North Sea

Durham
Rievaulx
Hereford
Cambridge
Exeter Oxford
Canterbury
Tournai
Deutz
Le Bec Paris Cologne Erfurt
St-Evroult Reims Heidelberg
Chartres
Angers Orléans Morimond
Tours Cluny
Kraków
Vienna
Buda
Cahors
Grenoble Vicenza Treviso Pécs
Toulouse Orange Padua
Palencia Huesca Avignon Bologna
Valladolid Montpellier Pisa Florence
Coimbra Salamanca Siena
Lisbon Lerida Perugia
Toledo Rome
Monte Cassino
Seville Salerno

Atlantic Ocean

Mediterranean Sea

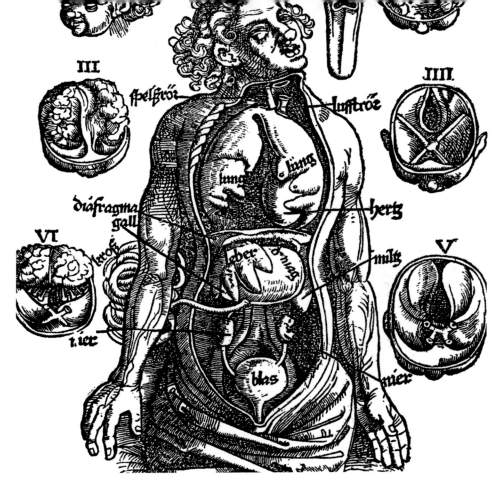

Labels on illustration: III, spelbröz, luftröz, IIII, lung, lung, hertz, diafragma, gall, VI, leber, magen, miltz, V, t.ier, blas, nier

Medicine and anatomy were developing sciences during this period, but dissection retained a certain taboo. For the most part, only those who had died at the hands of an executioner were handed over to anatomists, a practice that continued into the 19th century.

down 158 questions on theological problems alongside selections from Christian and pagan writers both for and against the proposition, as an invitation to apply logical thought to theology. Even at the end of his life, as an exiled monk, he retained his enthusiasm for this dialectical method and a suspicion of orthodoxy. The title of his final work says it all: *Dialogue between a Philosopher, a Pagan and a Jew.*

Universities

Abelard's approach was refined and developed by the greatest theologian of the Middle Ages, a 13th-century Dominican professor at the University of Paris called Thomas Aquinas. His *Summa Theologiae* represents the pinnacle of medieval humanism. But the fact that St Thomas had a logical tradition to develop, or a university at which to be a professor, owed much to the advances, struggles, and downright hubris of Abelard. His name did much for the reputation of 12th-century Paris as a font of learning and hotbed of new ideas at a time when advanced education was a disparate affair. The schools of particular towns might be known for particular specializations, but there was no coherent standard. As with so much else, these were thrown into sharp relief by the struggles between empire and papacy. As early as 1158, Frederick Barbarossa had conferred his pro-

tection upon the scholars of Bologna, "by whose knowledge [of Roman law] the world is illuminated in obedience to God and us, his ministers, and the life of his subjects is shaped" – i.e. a thick veneer of political theory would do the Empire no harm at all.

The reforming papacy, with its stress on a literate priesthood and its grounding in canon law, needed its own proponents and turned increasingly to the cathedral schools of Paris. King Philip Augustus had granted a charter to the nascent university in 1200, but Pope Innocent III went further to grant its scholars the right to elect their own officials in 1215, freeing them from clerical control. Governments, too, needed ever increasing numbers of trained officials, and this tripartite fostering of education brought the schools of various towns together, in an organic and unsystematic manner, as universities (the word then meant something similar to guild). Over the 12th century, the student seeking education as a path to riches became a favourite target of satirists. The idea that academia was a trade in itself, which produced a valuable commodity, learning, did not gain much momentum until the next century. By the 14th century, the idea had caught on, and rival German dynasties sought to outdo each other in the foundation of universities at Prague, Vienna, and elsewhere.

Literature

The spoken, written, and sung word were closely related in the Middle Ages. All three overlapped and intertwined in legal, church, courtly, and learned circles. Just as many theological treatises had their origin in public debates, so also much chivalric literature was born of heroic folk tales. It is telling that the most famous literary epic of the period is known as a song – the *Chanson de Roland*.

An image of troubadours playing for two princesses from the Canticles of St Mary, *attributed to Alfonso X of Léon-Castile (1252–84). Although heavily influenced by French and German notions of chivalry, the most vibrant theme of Spanish troubadours' tales at this time was the exploits of the great 11th-century general Rodrigo Diaz de Vivar, better known as El Cid.*

The imprisoned Boethius is consoled by Philosophy while Fortune turns her wheel. This 15th-century illumination encapsulates many of the concerns of scholarly literature on the eve of the Renaissance - classical learning, sorrow at man's lot, fate, and the cycle of life. At the top of Fortune's wheel is a king, at the bottom a fool.

Taverns and courts

About 100 troubadours are known by name from the century after 1150, including some 20 women. They were heirs of a rich tradition of story-telling and composition. Certain chansons from Spain combine Arabic and Hebrew elements with an early Spanish dialect. The majority draw upon the romantic doctrines of the Angevin courts, English nostalgia for the past, and Celtic mythology. In time, an increasing self-consciousness on the part of educated noble patrons created an environment in which different strands of tales and songs were woven together into courtly romances (the word means simply that they were composed in a vernacular Romance language). About 100 survive from the century after 1150, of which the most famous and accomplished were by Marie de France, Chrétien de Troyes, and Gautier d'Arras. The so-called "Matter of Britain", the body of stories about King Arthur, Lancelot, Perceval, and the Grail, was the favoured topic and Chrétien its master. His epics *Erec*, *Perceval*, *Yvain*, and others are sweeping canvases intended to excite, educate, and, to an extent, rehabilitate the aristocracy.

The other great epic tradition of the Middle Ages, of similarly rich and organic heritage, came from further north and east. The Scandinavian sagas were centuries old when they were first written down in the 13th century by the historian Snorri Sturlson and others. Filled with a deep, unsentimental pessimism in which man, the gods, and nature are all cruel, they tell of the wars of gods among themselves, giants and dragons, and the appalling sacrifices made by Odin, father of the gods, in his search for ultimate knowledge. By turns macabre, funny, and moving, they provide an impressive self-portrait of a people generally marginalized in studies of European culture, and prefigure much visionary and apocalyptic literature of the later medieval West. The *Nibelungenlied*, the great Germanic heroic epic that inspired Wagner's *Ring* cycle, tells a similarly bleak tale of a lost people and broken pantheon doomed by a woman's hatred.

If in Western Europe even mythical literary epics had deep Christian overtones, further east they were more scarce, if not absent.

Dante

Dante Alighieri was born in Florence in 1265. Like most Florentine nobles, his family were supporters of the Guelf party, a papal faction in origin, although by this time local concerns carried more weight. He

married, but subsequently fell in love with another young noblewoman, Beatrice. Although she died in 1290, he idealized her as a model of virtue and courtesy for the rest of his life. In 1300, the Guelf party split in two, and Dante found himself on the wrong side of political power. In 1302, he was convicted on trumped-up charges of embezzlement and anti-papalism and exiled from his beloved Florence. His magnificent *Divine Comedy* was forged in these fires of love and hatred.

The Divine Comedy centres on one pilgrim's journey, Dante's own, to God, through hell, purgatory, and finally paradise, drawn on by the agency of Beatrice. The reader is intended to understand that the pilgrim's journey is that of Everyman and that God will aid Everyman as he has the pilgrim, but Dante's vision of redemption is by turns apocalyptic and damning. He is just as concerned with those who are not redeemed as those who are. Of the 79 named people Dante encounters in his hell, 32 were Florentines. Only four made it as far as purgatory and only two to paradise. Popes and emperors fared no better than the common person. In Dante's heaven, there are outbursts against Pope Clement V and the Curial Church. The Knights Templar, recently suppressed, receive a staunch defence, as do the Franciscan friars, much persecuted for their overt poverty. Thomas Aquinas sits in heaven, but he sings the praises of the almost heretical Siger of Brabant, a scourge of recent orthodoxy. There are few heretical ideas that Dante does not incorporate in this deeply symbolic work of poetry. As much as *The Divine Comedy* is an elaborate vision of a new heaven and a new earth, it is also a celebration of Dante's native language. Language is not secondary to meaning, and, in Dante's work, Italian achieved a depth and articulation unparalleled in the Middle Ages.

Carmina Burana

Carmina Burana was the name given to a 13th-century manuscript containing 300 or so poems and lyrics, unearthed in a Benedictine library at Beuron, near Munich, by its first editor in 1847. Today the name is best known through Carl Orff's exuberant settings of some 20 of the poems for choir and orchestra, but its importance extends further: it is the largest and most varied surviving anthology of medieval Latin poetry written by the last poets to use that language as fluently as they did their native tongues. Within a few generations, their themes – love, drinking, gaming, adventure, and satire – were to be written almost exclusively in the vernacular. No subject is too high or too low for the *Carmina*. The best known, both because of Orff's famous opening and countless medieval illuminations, concerns Dame Fortune turning her wheel, "O how Fortune … apes

Geoffrey Chaucer

Born around 1343, the son of a London vintner, Geoffrey Chaucer led a colourful life. He was a prisoner of war in France, controller of customs in London, Knight of the Shire for Kent, and a deputy forester in Somerset. He was also the most prolific and versatile writer of his time. He produced plays, the standard treatise on the astrolabe, and a translation of Boethius' *Consolation of Philosophy,* but is best known for *The Canterbury Tales.* These sharp and often irreverent caricatures of a group of pilgrims en route to the shrine of Thomas à Becket at Canterbury are full of unparalleled insights into medieval life, both grand and mundane.

the moon's inconstancy: waxing, waning, losing, gaining … Life treats us detestably." Others, less contemplative, list the noises made by all known animals or the erotic speculations of men in taverns.

The Paston library

Even at the close of the Middle Ages, printing was rare and expensive, and the circulation of books necessarily constrained. Nonetheless, the library catalogues of noble households suggest that much epic, romance, and history was read. The library of one Sir John Paston gives some indication of what a 15th-century English gentleman's library might contain. He had Chaucer's *Troilus and Criseyde*, a chronicle of England to the reign of Edward III, Cicero's *On Friendship* and *On Old Age*, a book of knighthood, a book of heraldry, and a book on the death of Arthur, among many other titles. The number of books a man possessed is no real guide to the range of his reading, as many items might be gathered together in a single volume. Paston referred to his "Great Book", a compendium so similar to others known in later medieval England as to suggest that it was a standard collection readily available at any stationers for a reasonable price. Medieval Europe had its coffee table books, sumptuous illuminated Grail romances and so forth, but it also had its budget paperbacks.

Architecture

Grand architecture in the Middle Ages was a result of conflicting forces. Medieval cathedrals stand as supreme acts of praise – we can only imagine what went through the mind of a mason embarking on his stupendous task with only chisels, pulleys, and scaffolding. But those same cathedrals are also symbols of hubris. Conquering kings left magnificent cathedrals in their wakes – a clear message for all to read.

The Torre del Mangio, completed by 1341, dominates Siena, outstripping even the cathedral in height. It forms part of the town-hall complex of the central piazza, the Campo, which housed the communal government known as the Noveschi (the Nine). It was situated so as not to favour any one district of the city.

Romanesque churches were drenched with colour and detail. Altars, screens, fonts, columns, and archways commonly featured decorative or allegorical designs and images. Decorated capitals are particularly intriguing: despite their inconspicuous situation, they were as richly worked as any stone in the church. This example comes from the Cathedral at Pamplona in Spain.

From Romanesque to Gothic

The beginning of this period saw a great architectural expansion both in the number and the scale of buildings. Magnificent though Charlemagne's palatine chapel at Aachen was (built *c*.805), it was dwarfed by the churches built by kings and emperors in the 10th and 11th centuries. Most came to adopt an almost classical style now known as Romanesque. Almost always cross-shaped, and generally having an apse at the east end, their naves and roofs were supported by comparatively plain, round-headed arches. Windows were few and small, but engravings and paintings were many and rich. Grand examples are the cathedrals of St Martin of Tours and Santiago de Compostela. Uniquely, in Germany, cathedrals of the time often had two choirs, perhaps referring to the twin powers of Church and state united under imperial patronage. The best examples are the three imperial cathedrals, Speyer, Worms, and Mainz. Elsewhere, many small local churches still bear the characteristic decorative motifs of interlocking beaked heads and a zigzag design around their doors and windows. But as scholarly interest in the divine mechanics of the universe increased in the 12th century, so architects began to experiment, albeit often piecemeal, with a new style that reached for the heavens and gathered in the stars. Gothic architecture, as it was disparagingly termed by artists of the classicizing Renaissance, adopted intricate vaults of the type first seen in Durham Cathedral in 1104 and tall, pointed arches, typical of church architecture in Burgundy, to raise roofs high above the congregation and clear the way for soaring windows, creating cathedrals of light. The combination of artistry and trigonometric ingenuity that was so much part of the Gothic movement is encapsulated in its most typical feature, the flying buttress, which allowed higher, more delicate walls and greater apertures than ever before. The best examples today are Notre Dame Cathedral, Chartres Cathedral and the monastic

church of Mont St Michel. The first complete Gothic church was that of the Cathedral of St-Etienne in Sens, the archbishop of which, Henri Sanglier (1122–42), has a strong claim to be numbered among the great architectural innovators of the Middle Ages, but the Gothic style will forever be associated with Abbot Suger of St Denis.

Architecture and society

From the late 1130s, Abbot Suger began an extensive programme of rebuilding the ancient church of the Abbey of St Denis, near Paris, in a new, invigorating style. He wrote two very influential and widely circulated books that explained his architectural agenda and justified his endeavours. There is no doubting Suger's godliness, but nor is there any doubting his worldliness. St Denis was the patron saint of the relatively lowly Capetian kings of France. Suger was an influential royal adviser. Can it be a coincidence that the rebuilding of the abbey church was conceived immediately after the Capetian king Louis VI had brought the French nobility together with unprecedented success to face down the German Emperor Henry V? In Suger's account, St Denis himself miraculously aided the construction work, thus sealing the project with a holy approval that would have given much credibility to the Capetian dynasty. A complex political reality underlay the architectural advances of this relatively unimportant suburb, and the association of the steady expansion of Capetian power beyond the Ile de France with the expansion of Gothic architecture is striking.

Not everyone approved of lavish construction work. St Bernard of Clairvaux railed against those, especially the Cluniacs, who devoted money and energy to excessive projects, which were hardly in keeping with the simplicity of the monastic lifestyle. The grandeur of the church at Cluny suggests that he had a point. Bernard's own order, the Cistercians, developed a distinctive, restrained architectural style that, for a few decades at least, was uniform throughout its houses, from Fountains in England to Fontenay in France. Elsewhere, architecture sought to give far more explicit instruction. The bas-relief at Amiens Cathedral shows a noblewoman kicking a servant in the belly. A huge stone ox stands high on the towers of Laon Cathedral as a tribute to the nobility of the animal world, appreciated more by humanists than ever before. Monks appear in the guise of voracious wolves devouring sheep, Jews are shown as pigs, and women appear in all forms from Queen of Heaven to devils suckling toads.

Architecture and the state

The use of architecture as a means of propaganda reached its apogee in the Italian city-states, of which

The construction of the cathedral at Chartres, begun in 1194, signalled the beginning of the elaborate style known as High Gothic. Architectural patronage was very important. The statues and windows of the south portal, pictured here, were paid for by Peter of Dreux, Count of Brittany.

Siena is the most powerful example. There, the whole city was subordinated to a grand design for communal living by the detailed planning regulations of the *Noveschi*, the communal government. Fortified towers built by the various leading families were subject to height restrictions, and, from 1297, all buildings on the central square were forced to conform to a certain architectural design: columns were mandatory, but balconies forbidden. An elaborate scheme of city-wide public fountains was begun the next year. Siena's principal public building, the Palazzo Publico, itself housed the most overtly political piece of art in any of the Italian city-states: Ambroglio Lorenzetti's frescoes on the themes of good and bad government in the government's meeting room contained allegories on justice, the common good, and tyranny.

It was not (quite) all politics in the Italian city-states. The best known and most influential architectural artist of the communes was Giotto. Born of peasant background at the end of the 13th century, his work contains not only anti-imperial imagery (seen in the frescoes in the Scrovegni Chapel, Padua), but also narratives of the lives of two famous ascetics, St Francis and St John the Baptist (seen in the Church of Santa Croce, Padua). Perhaps Giotto was commissioned to rub out the taint of money which successful patrons of art in the city-states inevitably acquired.

The Roots of Renaissance

The Renaissance is generally thought to have begun around 1450, but it is easier to identify what its characteristics were not, than what they were. It was not just a renewed interest in classical art and scholarship, nor a sudden rejection of medieval views, values, and beliefs. Almost any aspect of the Renaissance can be prefigured in medieval Europe.

A 14th-century manuscript of Dante's Divine Comedy *picturing the Florentine poet together with Virgil, his guide, in hell with the damned. In his thinking on the relationships between religion, philosophy, and art, and his celebration of the learning of the classical world, Dante prefigured much that is generally associated with the 15th-century Renaissance.*

Calumny of Apelles, *Botticelli. Sandro Botticelli was the most individual and perhaps most influential artist in Florence at the end of the 15th century. It is likely that he had a member of the ruling Medici family as his patron. It is generally felt that the classical gods and heroes in his work are not carefree Olympians, but symbolic embodiments of some deep moral or metaphysical truth.*

Learning

The new learning of the 15th century possessed three more or less novel features, all related. First, it cultivated many classical authors well known today, but almost ignored by scholars of the Middle Ages, particularly Cicero and Homer. Secondly, ancient Greek played an increasingly prominent role in scholarship, parallel with Latin. Thirdly, biblical scholarship moved away from the extremes of symbolic interpretation to concentrate on linguistic studies of the original Hebrew and Greek texts. At the forefront of this new learning was a Dutchman called Gerhard Gerhards, better known by his Latin and Greek pen names, Desiderius and Erasmus. A regular visitor to London and Cambridge, he did more than any other scholar to unite scientific study of the classics and scripture with the Catholic tradition of the medieval church. His heyday coincided with the dawn of widespread printing and his *In Praise of Folly* ran to 43 editions in his lifetime.

Anti-clericalism

Though the Renaissance was not an abandonment of Catholic Christianity, it was a rejection of many of its trappings. In answer to his own question, "What would happen if the pope imitated Christ in his poverty?", Erasmus said "thousands of scribes, sycophants and pimps would go out of business". Similar denunciations had been uttered earlier in the Middle Ages by such "heretical" groups as the Waldensians; however, in the 15th century, increasing emphasis on the direct relationship between the individual and God without the need for a priest as intercessor or confessor – what was to become Protestantism – brought much clerical ritual under attack. At times this erupted into acts of iconoclasm, but for the most part it meant that the power of the Church was gradually limited to its religious concerns. Pope Gregory VII's 400-year-old dreams of a papal monarchy were slowly consigned to oblivion, and religion increasingly became a matter for private conscience.

Florence is still defined by its late medieval skyline. Its towers, now much admired for their architectural splendour, then housed warring factions of the sort that Dante found himself caught up in. It is an odd phenomenon that Florence produced so many renowned artists whereas the neighbouring Siena, equally prosperous, produced so few.

Science and society

As a result of the Church's diminishing authority over the secular world, scientists and philosophers were able to explore new ideas with less fear of censure. It was felt at this time that the secrets of the universe could be revealed by God-given ingenuity. This is not so very far from the advances made by 12th- and 13th-century scholars such as Abelard, John of Salisbury, and Thomas Aquinas. However, their interest had been in what the divine in man could reveal through introspection and logical thought, rather than in what the intellect could prise open.

The foremost quality of the Renaissance has been seen as independence of mind, and none possessed it as abundantly as Leonardo da Vinci. Born in 1452, he is best known for his paintings, particularly the *Mona Lisa* and the *Last Supper*. But painting was only ever a hobby; his principal interests were science and mechanics. Among the many unrealized designs in his notebooks were the machine gun, helicopter, and submarine.

World view

The Renaissance will always be thought of in terms of its great scientific thinkers – Leonardo, Galileo, Copernicus, and Bacon – but as with any great intellectual revolution, their thoughts hardly accorded with prevailing ideas about the world. This was still the age of astrology, alchemy, and magic. Nonetheless, the idea that humanity was capable of mastering the world in which it lived was growing, and the importance of Providence waning. The chains of sin weighed less heavily upon Renaissance thinkers than many of their predecessors, and in large part their achievement was not the conquest of new intellectual territory, but the overcoming of old fears.

One indication of this shift is the increasing reference to Europe, rather than Christendom. Of course, medieval scholars had known that they lived on a continent called Europe by classical geographers, but for many their knowledge of the world beyond their own locality came from tales of martyrs, pilgrims, and crusaders. During the course of the Middle Ages, the idea that Christendom was a common fold for the peoples of Europe had suffered many erosions. Princes had bought off popes. An ecumenical conference of 1439 in Florence allowed the Catholic and Greek Orthodox Churches to take a good look at each other and realize just how different they were. The "Christendom of Europe", as one priest put it in 1572, was being pushed ever westwards. The Ottoman conquests of the East prevented it from ever returning.

The Ebstorf map (c.1283). Not all
medieval maps were created for
practical purposes. Often they were
intended to show the symbolic
importance of Jerusalem as the centre of
a flat world and Christ as its ruler. That
is not to say that there was no such skill
as cartography – many medieval maps
of Europe could guide a fairly tolerant
traveller today.

THE CHURCH AND BELIEF

Looking back at the Middle Ages today, we can see far more of the broad trends than contemporaries ever could, but almost nothing of personal life. For the most part, belief can only be traced through its institution, the Church. Seen in that distant mirror, faith drove people to seek the earthly Jerusalem on pilgrimage and crusade, and it gave popes the authority to meld a monarchy out of the bishopric of Rome.

Heaven and hell

Medieval art produced many striking images of heaven and hell. For most people a painting above a church altar of the Devil, horned, winged, and bathed in fire, was far more immediate than any words of scripture a priest might read beneath it. The physical torments of Dante's *Inferno* were as imminent as the physical blessings of his *Paradise*, so much so that the 12th-century German bishop Otto of Freising reminded his readers that descriptions of the afterlife in scripture were not necessarily to be taken literally. From the late 12th century, the geography of the otherworld gained a new continent. The idea that there might be a state between salvation and damnation had been considered likely by the Church fathers, but it was not until after 1170 that purgatory was recognized as a place where venial sins were punished between death and the Last Judgement. In *The Divine Comedy*, although its torments are no less horrendous, purgatory is a happier place than hell because it has hope of eventual redemption. The notion of purgatory brought with it huge spiritual motivation, not just to be faithful, but also to be obedient. In the course of the Middle Ages, a fourth region emerged. Unbaptized children and worthy souls who had never known Christ because they lived before His time or where His teaching had not yet reached were consigned to Limbo, a state without punishment, but with no possibility of redemption. There Dante finds Homer, Plato, and Aristotle as well as the Muslim general Saladin.

Jerusalem as the centre of the world

More often than not, medieval maps did not have any practical agenda. Instead, they sought to show the fundamental importance of Jerusalem, both literally and symbolically, by placing it at the centre of the world. The literal and symbolic were united in 1099 when the holy city was recaptured from Islam during the First Crusade. The author of one chronicle describes the tomb of Christ as "the navel of the world".

The range of belief

The Middle Ages are generally spoken of as "an age of faith", but perhaps things were not so clear cut. First impressions are of the incredible wealth of the Church, the grandeur of its buildings, and the nature of surviving documents. But the ecclesiastical writers who shape our conception of the medieval world were not just writing for us, they were also writing for their contemporaries who might very well have needed cajoling with pious imprecations and a few plainly stated examples.

Architects and their patrons knew perfectly well that magnificent churches reinforced the majesty of God, as well as reflecting it. A cynic might note how many more representations of judgement there are in medieval church art than of salvation. Genuine faith shaped belief, but so did politics, varying interpretations of scripture, convenience, vice, and doubt. As a consequence, the medieval Church was far more accommodating than usually assumed. King Henry I of England acknowledged more than 20 illegitimate children, but after his death chroniclers remembered his reign as a peaceful one blessed by God. His brother, William Rufus, was remembered in no such terms, but then he took little trouble to hide his total contempt for matters of the Church. There is a place for religious scepticism in our thinking about the Middle Ages.

The Monastic Orders

Economic and political concerns could easily intrude upon the contemplative life. As a result, many monastic houses looked to strict regulations to preserve their way of life. The most influential was Benedict's Rule, drawn up by St Benedict of Nursia for the monastery of Monte Cassino in the early 6th century. Three hundred years later, St Benedict of Aniane fostered its implementation across Christendom.

Benedictine monasticism

The guiding principle of Benedict's Rule was humility in all things. The particulars of humility, in terms of the consumption of food, drink, sleep, and the regular duties of monks, were spelled out in detail. Implicit in Benedict's concept of humility was total obedience to one's superior; in the case of a monk, his abbot. Should the abbot demand an impossible act, the monk was to explain, meekly, why this was so, but if the abbot insisted, then the monk was to trust in God and obey. Humility was also to be learnt by daily toil in the fields, between the many hours of meticulously timetabled prayer and worship. Above all, the Rule was a sensible one for communal living. It ordained that monks should sleep in separate beds within a dormitory; bedclothes varied according to a monk's age and health. Instructions were given for the care of the sick. Food was to be frugal but adequate, and monks were to prepare it each in turn.

Benedict's Rule was profoundly important, but its focus was inwards. Monasteries remained part of the world, often dependent on some form of secular sponsorship or support, or falling under the sway of a local bishop who might himself have a political agenda. An awareness of this led to a period of intensive and radical monastic reform in the 10th century. The Burgundian monastery of Cluny, founded in 909, was placed beyond the interference of any but the pope by its founder, William of Aquitaine. Through Cluny's example, and its ever increasing number of dependent houses, the idea that outside interference was undesirable gained currency not just among monks but among lay men as well. No wonder that for the century or so following 1050 Cluny and the reforming papacy enjoyed such good relations.

The new orders

Cluny's successes were overt. It gathered about itself an almost feudal network of nearly 1500 dependent

Cluny, as it appears today. When the Norman knight William of Warenne came to Cluny at the end of the 11th century, fresh from the conquest of England, he would have encountered a similar complex. He and his wife were so impressed by the Cluniac order that they begged the abbot to send some monks to join them in England. This he did, and a small Cluniac priory was founded in Lewes, Sussex.

This 15th-century illumination shows St Bernard teaching in a Dominican house. This event could never have occurred – St Bernard died half a century before the Dominican movement got underway – but it shows the close association that came to be perceived between the intellectual rigour for which St Bernard was famed and the Dominican Order, which increasingly sunk its roots in the universities.

smaller monasteries across Germany, Spain, Italy, and France, and encouraged wealthy sinners to repent by donating their goods to its houses. It emphasized pilgrimage as a means of penitence and placed its authority behind a number of high-profile schemes to limit aristocratic warmongering – including the Peace and Truce of God – which restricted knightly violence to certain activities and certain times. Consequently Cluny became very much part of the pious noble's way of life. It even encouraged "lay brothers" to join its ranks and tend its fields as a partial commitment to a monastic life. For all its many merits, by the early 12th century, Cluny had become far more wordly than its early abbots had ever intended.

Towards the end of the 11th century, Bruno of Cologne, a former master of theology at Rheims, established a rule and community of monks at La Chartreuse, high in the Alps. Their houses were rough and ready, their diet intensely meagre, their shirts often woven of hair. In fact, their only extravagance was a rich library. Such was the withdrawal from the world of what was to become the Carthusian order that its monks met with each other only a few times each week, and water was piped to each monk's cell to limit accidental encounters. Elsewhere, at Citeaux in Burgundy, a disenchanted Cluniac monk, Robert of Molesme, had established a house according to his own austere principles. Robert himself returned to the Cluniacs, but his foundation prospered to become the home of the Cistercian order. Seeking to return to the letter of St Benedict's Rule, the community devoted a fixed part of each day to manual labour. It is a fitting irony that, as the Middle Ages wore on, the Cistercian order gained a reputation for large-scale cultivation and land management.

Bernard of Clairvaux

The Cistercians came to be more widespread and influential than any other order. Preferring remote sites where they could be alone and self-sufficient – such as Fountains, Rievaulx, and Tintern in England – they became masters of civil engineering in desolate river valleys. They were fortunate in having a series of dynamic abbots. The third abbot, Stephen Harding, compared Cistercian copies of scripture with those housed elsewhere and, in consultation with native speakers of Hebrew, sought to produce an authoritative version. Most important, however, because of his many influential and widespread writings, was St Bernard of Clairvaux. He joined the Cistercians in 1113 and founded his famous house at Clairvaux in 1115. By the time of his death in 1153, it had 65 daughter houses.

On reading some of the many surviving letters of St Bernard, one could be forgiven for thinking that he wanted to turn the whole world into Citeaux, as seen in his exchanges with his friend William of St Thierry concerning Cluniac architecture, or his attacks on the pomp of Peter Abelard. But in addition to his constant engagement with the key spiritual questions of the time, his great ability was in finding a path for those who could not submit wholly to the cloistered life. He encouraged his friend St Norbert in his establishment of the Premonstratensian Canons, who were to be partly monastic, partly active, and partly apostolic. He was also a staunch supporter of the new military orders formed in Jerusalem in the 12th century for the defence of the kingdom. For all the wrong reasons, these orders – the Knights Templar and Knights Hospitaller – are better known today than any other monastic order.

Heretics, Mystics, and Friars

The monastic ideal was a simple life of spiritual toil, lived out in a community which offered mutual support, provided structure, and limited excess. For some this did not go far enough – the monastery brought its own temptations. Others found certain teachings of the Catholic Church unacceptable. This was as much a time of charismatic dissenters as it was of orthodox teachers. The friction between them was a seismic force.

1000–1400

THE MIDDLE AGES

Asceticism

In the Middle Ages, an obvious means of asserting one's holy credentials was in great acts of physical privation and spiritual resolution. In the first few centuries of Christianity, feats of endurance had become almost a spiritual industry. St Macarius of Alexandria, for example, could not bear to be outdone and would seek to better any act of self-denial. He never matched the performance of St Symeon the Stylite, who stood unprotected on top of a pillar for 33 years. St Daniel was made of yet sterner stuff and bested him by three months. For many, this ostentatious withdrawal from the world of the flesh, in its milder forms at least, had a more obvious spiritual currency than popes on their thrones and bishops in their palaces. Not only did it offer inspiration to souls searching spiritual solace, but it also provided a ready weapon with which protesters could attack the perceived errors and excesses of the established Church.

Heresy

In the medieval Church, those who followed a religion other than Christianity were pitied or derided as schismatics. Heresy, however, was in the eye of the beholder. Over the centuries, certain sects had indeed placed themselves in clear opposition to the central precepts of Christianity, but many preachers, who perhaps saw themselves in the mould of Elijah or John the Baptist, found their teaching branded heretical by popes who felt them too close, or too far, for comfort. It was an easy trap to fall into, and it caught many who did little more than rock a bishop's boat. In the early 12th century, Arnold of Brescia, a man of educated and noble background, preached a return to apostolic simplicity and was condemned by Pope Innocent II for his troubles. Later in the 12th century, a merchant from Lyons called Peter Waldo chose to do as St Matthew advised and sold his goods to give to the poor. He embarked on a life of preaching, translating the scriptures into the vernacular to aid him in his task. As a broadly anti-clerical layman, teaching and interpreting the Word, he and his followers, the Waldensians, a movement practising extreme humility, teetered on the edge of condemnation for many years.

Most damaging to the medieval Church was the Cathar movement. The Cathar answer to why there was evil in a world created by a good God was a simple but drastic extension of Christian belief: a Light God reigned over the spiritual world, but a Dark God presided over the physical. Such a belief came very close to denying the incarnation of God and the possibility of His redeeming the world, but its simple answers to questions of injustice and the human condition appealed to many who felt little affinity with bejewelled bishops and mercenary monks. Cathar preachers roamed the countryside in pairs, dissociating themselves from the physical world by ever greater degrees of deprivation and gaining ever more converts, especially among the villages and lesser nobility of southern France. Perhaps the greatest catalyst to the movement's success was that it welcomed women as active participants.

Friars

The medieval Church had little answer to these attacks. Many popular movements for poverty such as the Waldensians overtly practised what they

A grisly illustration of the Knights Templar being burned at the stake following their condemnation by Philip IV of France between 1307 and 1314. The illustration comes from a 14th-century manuscript of the World Chronicle *by Bernard Guy, the most infamous of the Dominican inquisitors.*

Giotto's fresco of St Francis of Assisi preaching to the birds from the Upper Church at Assisi, Italy. The fresco cycle at Assisi portrays the establishment view of St Francis and the friars. Following the papal line, it very much underplays the extent to which Francis felt unease at the increasingly institutional nature of the order.

preached. Some had become intertwined with those parts of society with which the Church had little contact, particularly the urban poor. It was perhaps in recognition of this fact that Pope Innocent III and in particular Cardinal Ugolino, the future Pope Gregory IX, were so keen to foster and encourage the activities of a young merchant from Assisi who, at the beginning of the 13th century, renounced all worldly goods to preach and care for the sick.

St Francis of Assisi is one of the best-known and most charismatic figures of the Middle Ages, which is just how his official biographers wanted it. Within a few years of his revelation, he had acquired a small group of followers, the *fratres minor* (little brothers), or friars, and written a simple Rule for their lives. At the heart of their existence was poverty. The friars were to be homeless, begging for the smallest amount necessary to keep body and soul together. Although Francis met with the most powerful men of his time, even trying to convert the Egyptian sultan al-Kamil, he never accepted that any good could come of money. He wished to die a hermit, but his example was too useful a one to be allowed to pass unnoticed. When Ugolino became pope, he ordained that the Franciscan order could hold property and buildings by means of a third party to aid in its orga-

nization and propagation. Step by step, the papacy remodelled the original order into a spiritual powerhouse from which St Francis would have recoiled.

Francis considered knowledge to be a form of property, which was not a view shared by his contemporary Dominic of Guzman. St Dominic was also of a wealthy background, and, having acquired a first-rate education, he, too, renounced his material wealth. During the first two decades of the 13th century, he wandered the Midi region of France as a pauper, preaching in particular to Cathars. Where others had failed, his poverty and austerity allowed him to succeed.

Dominic and his small group of followers came to the attention of Innocent III, who recognized the potential of educated but unworldly preachers and supported Dominic in his establishment of the order that bears his name. By 1219, he had set up houses in Paris, Bologna, Rome, Madrid, and Seville. Two years later, Dominic himself succumbed to the rigours of his self-imposed lifestyle. Fifty years later there were 450 Dominican priories across Europe. The Dominicans became prominent in the universities and were often called upon to provide official theologians; because of this they were to become the order in charge of the Inquisition.

Pilgrimage

In 1026, Duke Richard II of Normandy together with Abbot Richard of St Vanne set out for the Holy Land. A six-month journey brought them to Jerusalem on Palm Sunday 1027. Holy Week was spent visiting the sites of Christ's Passion, culminating at Calvary where, according to the abbot's biographer, many tears were shed. It is easy to think of this as an elaborate public-relations exercise, but for many the tears were genuine. Pilgrimage had become an integral part of the religious life.

Relics

A pilgrimage to Jerusalem would have seemed infinitely remote to most people, but the physical remains of saints, together with items connected with the life and death of Christ, held a fundamental place in the fabric of medieval life. They could be found on altars to invoke blessing, in courts of law to guarantee oaths, and on the battlefield to confer protection. For many ordinary people, they were the main conduits of supernatural power. Particularly powerful were the relics of martyrs, the healing properties of which often bore a grisly relationship to the martyr's demises: the relics of a decapitated saint, for example, were held to be very good for headaches.

For religious communities, relics ensured both a sympathetic ear in heaven along with considerable prestige on earth, so much so that monks plundered tombs, raided other churches, and made dubious deals in the hope of acquiring a holy finger or toe. Not surprisingly, selling holy relics could be a lucrative business, and there was a good deal of deliberate fraud. The Pardoner in Chaucer's *Canterbury Tales* did rather well for himself selling pig's bones to the faithful, and Protestant reformers took great delight in counting how many fingers of St Peter were in circulation, for example, or speculating as to how large a galleon could be built from the fragments of the True Cross.

Penitence

Why would a pilgrim travel to see relics if St Peter's fingers were to be found throughout Europe? Certainly the relics of more highly placed saints were believed to possess a greater potency than their lesser brethren, and the closer a saint had been to Christ the greater their appeal. Thus Rome, which could claim St Peter and St Paul in addition to countless Christian martyrs, was second only to Jerusalem as a pilgrimage destination.

There was also a threefold penitential aspect to pilgrimage. First, journeys beyond the horizon were generally uncommon, and so pilgrimage was an arduous business that could stand simply as punishment for venial sins. Secondly, as this idea gained momentum, certain pilgrimages brought with them official Church indulgences – set amounts of time off purgatory for good behaviour – and different destinations could be rated against each other: three pilgrimages to Canterbury were "worth" one to Rome, which itself had to be visited twice to match Jerusalem. Thirdly, a saint might intercede with God, according to his or her own rank, to remit yet more sin. The great 12th-century church at Conques in France housed the (stolen) relics of a Roman martyr, Faith. A tympanum over the west door showed wonderfully horrific scenes of the Last Judgement, reminding the pilgrim that the intercession of St Faith was worth having. With that in mind, they might very well dig a little deeper in their pockets.

Santiago de Compostela

One element in the great success of the cult of St Faith, in all other respects a rather minor saint, was that Conques was on the Camino de Santiago (the Way of St James) – the great pilgrim road running from Le Puy in northern France to Compostela in north-west Spain. In the early 9th century, Bishop Diego of Compostela announced that he had uncovered the body of St James in his cathedral's foundations. The discovery was a happy one. St James was an apostle, the only member of Christ's inner circle whose relics were not known to reside anywhere else, and since the 7th century it was believed that St James had visited Spain. A steady trickle of pilgrims came to the shrine, which grew in importance in the 10th and 11th centuries. By the 12th century, Santiago de Compostela exerted a greater pull for pilgrims than anywhere other than Jerusalem and Rome. St James's cockle shell became a great mark of prestige and spiritual succour worn by successful pilgrims (or those who wished to appear so) for centuries to come. Compostela no longer had bishops; it had archbishops.

Santiago was closely associated with Cluny. The Burgundian house established dependent priories

Bardsey Island

Bardsey Island, just off the tip of the Lleyn Peninsula in Wales, was known in the Middle Ages as the Isle of 20,000 Saints, after the number of saints believed to be buried there. A prescribed pilgrimage route ran down the north coast of the peninsula from church to church, most of which housed their own relics. Almost unknown now, during the Middle Ages it was a site of national importance. Two pilgrimages to the island were the equivalent of one to Canterbury. In a wonderfully typical piece of medieval circularity, burial on Bardsey guaranteed that one became a saint.

and hostels along the Way of St James to put up weary pilgrims, many of which acquired their own relics and developed their own cults, until the Way became almost a package tour. Cluny also seems to have encouraged northern knights to travel to Spain to aid the border kingdoms of Navarre and Léon-Castile in their battles with Muslims who had annexed large parts of central and southern Spain in the 8th century. These knights bore the standard of St James.

Pilgrimage and crusade

When medieval writers referred to the events now known as the Crusades, they spoke only of armed pilgrimages. Crusaders, like pilgrims, received spiritual privileges – indulgences – which in the popular mind at least meant that those who died on crusade were guaranteed an immediate place in Heaven, their sins wiped clean. The idea of long, arduous penitential journeys was a necessary precursor to the preaching of any crusading ideas. More important still was the understanding that there was something of special and immediate importance about the Holy Land, even a millennium or more after Christ's ascension. Relics, too, played an important part in the development of a crusading ideology. In 1098, the Crusaders were besieged at Antioch by the army of Karbuqa, emir of Mosul. The situation was desperate until a group of soldiers from Provence were guided by a vision to discover in the Church of St Peter the lance that had pierced the side of the crucified Christ. The effect on morale was miraculous – what greater divine endorsement? – and three days later the Turkish army was routed.

The Crusades for the Holy Land

In early 1095, representatives of the Byzantine emperor Alexius I Comnenus appealed to Pope Urban II for military aid against the incursions of the Seljuk Turks into Asia Minor. In November, in a stage-managed showcase in Clermont in the Auvergne, Urban called Western Christendom to arms to reunite the Eastern and Western Churches.

1000–1400

THE MIDDLE AGES

A late 12th-century portrait of Saladin I, sultan of Egypt, from the Fatamid school of painting. Though "the enemy", Saladin was much admired in Western Christendom for his martial valour and personal nobility. In his Divine Comedy, *Dante placed him not in Hell, but in purgatory together with Virgil, Homer, and other virtuous non-Christians.*

Crusaders answered the call of Urban II from across Christendom, although most knights seem to have come from France, the Western Empire, and the Norman lands. The pope expected a single army to march, but in the event four almost independent professional armies formed, together with a fifth popular movement, each of which followed their own routes to Constantinople. They converged in the spring of 1097.

The origins of the crusading idea

The Crusades were responsible for fundamental changes in Western Europe. Not only did the movement of tens of thousands of men, women, horses, and their provisions to and from Palestine and the East necessitate a revolution in transport, finance, and government, but the Crusades also brought the world beyond the borders of Western Christendom more sharply into focus than ever before. Their effects are far easier to identify than their causes. Certainly, once under way, any large-scale military endeavour gathers its own momentum, but what initially inspired so very many people across Europe to answer the pope's call?

The events of 1095 were not wholly unexpected. Pope Gregory VII had thought he might lead his own expedition in 1074, and Western knights had been fighting the Arab world under the banner of the cross in southern Spain for many decades. The idea of a just or holy war had been gaining intellectual ground since the time of St Augustine, but it is unlikely to have penetrated popular consciousness. More influential was the long-established tradition of pilgrimage and veneration of the Holy Land, together with the popular movement known as the Peace and Truce of God. The Peace and Truce sought to place limits on knightly violence, forbidding it outright on certain holy days and under certain circumstances, offering a manageable compromise to many nobles who might otherwise have fallen under outright condemnation. In time, the Peace and Truce became the badge of honour of the knight of God. Urban II melded these ideas together to form a weapon and offered as added inducement remission of penances imposed by the Church in this lifetime to those who "took the cross". Fairly quickly this developed into

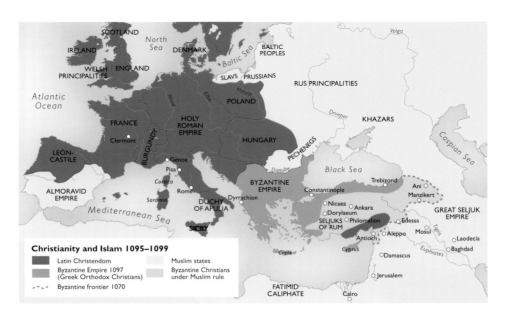

Christianity and Islam 1095–1099

- Latin Christendom
- Byzantine Empire 1097 (Greek Orthodox Christians)
- - - Byzantine frontier 1070
- Muslim states
- Byzantine Christians under Muslim rule

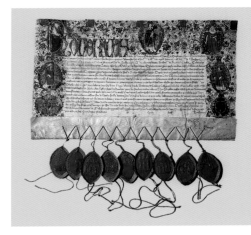

Indulgences

Indulgences, written grants which remitted penances or even bought off time in purgatory, were one of the principal rewards of pilgrims and crusaders, as was the case with this 15th-century German example. But many more were sold for profit by popes, bishops, and lesser scoundrels than ever rewarded the faithful. Pope Nicholas IV (1288–92) paid for most of his new church of Santa Maria Maggiore at Colonna, including elaborate mosaics, out of indulgence income, while pardoners, who sold fake indulgences to line their own pockets, were the butt of much medieval satire.

the idea that those who died on crusade went directly to heaven. In addition to this spiritual reward, there was the chance for unlimited plunder.

The First Crusade

Within a year of Urban's sermon at Clermont, expeditions were being prepared by some of the great lords of Europe, including Hugh, brother of King Philip I of France; Robert, Duke of Normandy; and Stephen, Count of Blois. They were joined by one of the most dynamic military leaders in Christendom, the Norman Bohemund, fresh from conquests in southern Italy. The first contingents reached Constantinople in November 1096, though huge numbers had been lost en route. By April 1097, the various crusading armies were camped outside Constantinople and starting to fight among themselves. Alexius sought to extract oaths of loyalty from these increasingly unwelcome guests, but ultimately the Crusades were more disastrous for Byzantium than the Muslim world.

Two years after they had gathered at Constantinople, in July 1099, the crusaders captured Jerusalem. It had taken two major battles at Dorylaeum and Antioch, and three long sieges at Nicaea, Antioch, and Jerusalem to bring them there, and they had suffered terrible losses. The expedition had done nothing to reunite the Eastern and Western Churches – if anything, it had fostered mutual distrust between Greece and Rome – but it had returned a large part of Asia Minor to Byzantium, and Westerners had carved out four states for themselves in the East: Edessa, Antioch, Jerusalem, and Tripoli. In the words of the chronicler Fulcher of Chartres, many poor people became extremely wealthy.

The Crusades to 1204

The establishment of the Crusader States committed Westerners to crusading for some time. The Second Crusade, launched in 1146, was a response to the conquest of Edessa by Zengi, Atabeg of Mosul, at Christmas 1144. Pope Eugenius III and King Louis VII of France sought to muster a response, but to no real avail. It took a lengthy preaching campaign by Bernard of Clairvaux to get the enterprise off the ground, rallying French, German, Spanish, and English leaders. Perhaps because it was initially so dependent on one man's charisma, once under way the Second Crusade was less able to withstand the horrors of war, and it suffered major defeats at Dorylaeum and Laodecia, almost collapsing in confusion. Only the discipline and determination of the Knights Templar saved the army from total defeat in the winter of 1147–8. Bernard was blamed for the failure of the Second Crusade, somewhat unjustly, but the real losers were the Franks settled and increasingly isolated in the Crusader States. By 1187, the brilliant sultan of Egypt, Saladin, had captured Jerusalem and Tripoli.

The Third Crusade, launched to recapture Jerusalem in 1190, was under the command of three kings, Richard the Lionheart of England, Philip II of France, and Frederick Barbarossa of Germany. None trusted the others, and so each planned meticulously for his own safety. Following some modest successes, Richard, by then the effective leader, made a three-year truce with Saladin in 1192. Hostilities were resumed under Pope Innocent III in 1198, and the Crusades were placed on an altogether more commercial footing. Venice financed the expedition on unfavourable terms, leaving the pope and Crusaders in debt. When the deposed Byzantine emperor Alexius Angelus offered the West vast sums of money to help him regain his throne, the possibilities of financial gain finally outstripped religious and even political motivation. On 13 April 1204, the crusaders breached the walls of Constantinople. The next three days were spent pillaging the richest city in the world.

The Other Crusades

In the late 11th century, Islam had been seen to present a threat on two fronts, both in the East and in the Iberian Peninsula. Pagan Slavs were targeted by the Second Crusade. The campaigns of Henry the Lion, Duke of Saxony, against the pagan Wends of the Baltic were granted crusade status by Pope Eugenius III in 1147. In 1209, Innocent III inaugurated the Albigensian Crusade against the Cathar heretics.

Spain

Not until 1113 did campaigning against Islam in the Iberian Peninsula earn the same indulgences as campaigning in the Holy Land, even though it had a far longer history. After the collapse of the Caliphate of Cordoba in 1002, Muslim Spain had broken up into a number of small emirates. The Christian kingdoms in the north were just as fragmentary, but, as they were poorer, they were less cultured and more militant than their Muslim neighbours. The first Christian ruler to take any action against Islam was Ferdinand I of Léon-Castile, conquering much of what was to become Portugal. After his death, his sons Sancho and Alfonso fought for the throne. Alfonso eventually emerged as ruler. He had as his general one of the best-known and most revered military leaders of Christendom, Rodrigo Diaz, known as El Cid, who carved out a principality for himself at Valencia and combined diplomacy and brilliant military tactics to limit Muslim reconquest. Alfonso captured Toledo in 1085, a great success, but after the death of El Cid in 1099 was unable to hold back the vast African army

of the Almoravid prophet-general Yusuf. The Christian initiative passed to Aragon, and, by the 1170s, the Christian kingdoms had regained some of their former strength. In the wake of setbacks in the East, the papacy took a renewed interest in the Iberian Peninsula. Under the sponsorship of the tireless and implacable Innocent III, the united forces of Navarre, Castile, and Aragon, supported by some French knights, inflicted a massive defeat on the Almohad Muslims under al-Nasir at Las Navas in 1206. This battle has traditionally been seen as the great watershed of Spanish medieval history.

The Albigensian Crusade

The initial response of the papacy to the growth of the Cathar heresy was one of preaching followed by excommunication, but the appeal of Catharism was too great and too entrenched, and the failings of many orthodox priests too obvious for this to have any long-term effect. Innocent III sent regular missions to Languedoc, the Cathar heartland, but clearly felt the frustration of a century and a half of reform-

An illustration of a battle between Christians and Muslims from the 14th-century Romance of Geoffrey of Bouillon. *Such conflicts were the single greatest formative influence upon the Iberian Peninsula in the Middle Ages, determining its territorial and political structure and cultural and religious outlooks for centuries to come.*

Montsegur in southern France, constructed as a Cathar stronghold at the beginning of the 13th century. Understandably, it was thought impregnable. When the castle finally fell to royalist forces in 1244, four generations of its lord's family were found there. As the Inquisition was to discover, Catharism was often a family affair with widely spread roots.

ing popes before him and became ever more militant in his language. He appealed initially to the French king, Philip II, then to the foremost French lords to back his words with force of arms, but it took the murder of a papal legate in Languedoc in 1208 to spur the French nobility into action.

In 1209, a crusade of troops from France and its neighbours swept down the Rhone to capture several Cathar strongholds; however, many, having completed the term for which they had signed up and got their time off purgatory, returned home. A new leader was chosen, the efficient and brutal Simon de Montfort, who managed to make enemies of most of the rulers of southern France. He killed in battle Peter II of Aragon, an orthodox ruler seeking only to defend his interests north of the Pyrenees. De Montfort himself was killed besieging Toulouse in 1218, and over the next six years the enterprise was beaten back. King Louis VIII of France led a second invasion in 1226, and three years later the south surrendered. The crusade had been as horrific as any of the Eastern ventures. The motto of one of its leaders is indicative of the crusaders' brutality: "kill them all, let God sort them out".

The Albigensian Crusade, named after the Cathar stronghold Albi, was unlike all others because it was directed against an internal enemy. As with the early Crusades, however, it highlighted the extent to which such undertakings were dependent on the abilities and charisma of their rulers and subject to those rulers pursuing their own interests. The lessons learnt in the early years of the Crusades led the Fourth Lateran Council of 1215 to lay down ordinances requiring the co-operation of secular powers in the fight against heresy. It also made provision for the Inquisition.

The Inquisition

The Inquisition was created by Pope Gregory IX in the early 13th century to seek out heretics and either bring them back within the fold of orthodoxy or punish their obstinacy. Inquisitors, for the most part Dominican friars because of their impeccable spiritual credentials and skills in doctrinal debate, followed set circuits in pairs. Upon arrival in a new region, they demanded that heretics be denounced or themselves come forward. The fear which will forever be associated with the Inquisition arose out of the fact that witnesses made their denunciations in private: communities could be destroyed quickly. A person denounced as a heretic had no legal defence, no knowledge of his accuser, and only a vague idea of what evidence had been brought against him. Torture came to play an increasing part in proceedings. For most, innocent or guilty, the only option was confession in the hope that the penance imposed would be bearable. Those who refused to admit guilt were deemed obdurate and handed over to the secular authorities for punishment. In some famous cases, they were burned alive. In the vast majority of cases, punishments were less brutal, and the accused lived to repent, in public at least. Nonetheless, for most individuals and communities, a visit from the Inquisition could mean only horror, suspicion, and pain.

The Great Schism

Boniface VIII (1294–1303) possessed all the characteristics of a medieval pope in abundance. He was very active in politics and was responsible for a significant contribution to the corpus of canon law and the Bull *Unam Sanctam*, an extreme assertion of papal supremacy. In 1303, he was kidnapped by an agent of the French king Philip IV and died in captivity. French pressure mounted, and six years later the papacy went into exile.

A contemporary illustration of a battle between Hussites and crusaders from the so-called Jena Codex. *Hus' followers were so enraged by his excommunication that they launched what was in effect a national uprising. In 1419, the pope announced a general crusade against them, but their popular base was too strong. Year after year, waves of German crusaders were defeated.*

The Great Schism of 1378-1417 divided Europe along political lines defined almost directly by the relationship of a particular country with France. Scotland, for instance, was often an ally of France in its conflicts with England, and hence threw such weight as it had behind the Avignon pope. England, on the other hand, preferred Rome for the same reason.

Exile

Thanks to the efforts of the French faction in Rome, Pope Clement V took the papacy into exile at Avignon in 1309. It finally returned to Rome under Gregory IX in 1377. Avignon itself was an independent papal enclave, but, whatever half-hearted notions of escaping politics were held, French influence was felt all around. All seven Avignon popes were Frenchmen elected by a French-dominated college of cardinals. Unsurprisingly, many of its decisions were made with French interests in mind. Most notorious was the trial and dissolution of the Knights Templar (1307–14), culminating in the public burning of the Grand Master, Jacques de Molai, pursued largely because of the vendetta of Philippe le Bel, grandson of King Louis IX.

Many countries were ambivalent in their attitude towards the Avignon papacy and its spiritual authority lost much credibility. Despite the threat of the Inquisition, ever more unorthodox sects sprang up across Europe, often following the model of the friars. The Franciscan Spirituals (Fraticelli), Beguines, and Friends of God all rejected property and the trappings of clerical religion, emphasizing instead mysticism and personal communion with God. Particularly influential were the teachings of the Czech John Hus and Englishman John Wycliffe. Wycliffe, an Oxford academic, denounced wealth, papal supremacy, and the doctrine of transubstantiation. His followers, the Lollards, formed the most widespread popular religious movement in medieval England. After his death, Wycliffe's body was exhumed and burnt for heresy. Hus, once head of the University of Prague, developed Wycliffe's ideas in Bohemia and became the focus for Czech resentment of the German hierarchy.

Schism

On its return to Rome in 1377, the College of Cardinals was politically riven and immediately managed to elect two men as pope simultaneously, Urban VI and Clement VII. There had been antipopes in the past, but never before had the papacy

so obviously brought such a scandal down on its own head. Over the next 30 years, neither man was moved to compromise, and both were given to atrocious reprisals against their opponents. Finally, in 1409 a third pope was elected by the increasingly desperate and terrified College of Cardinals. This situation persisted until 1414, when the German king Sigismund, with the support of the despairing Parisian professors, summoned all cardinals, bishops, abbots, friars, princes, and teachers to Constance to settle the matter. Eighteen thousand people answered his call.

The Council of Constance lasted three years. It brought the schism to an end by setting aside all three popes and electing unanimously in their place Cardinal Odo Colonna as Martin V (1417–31). The council sought to limit the power of the papacy over secular institutions, but it also burned John Hus as a destabilizing heretic. A further council to consider the

The Great Schism 1378–1417
Areas recognizing Rome-based pope
Areas recognizing Avignon-based pope
Centre of Hussite activity
Centre of Lollard activity

Wycliffe's Bible

For much of the Middle Ages, the Bible was only ever available in the Vulgate, i.e. Latin, version. To John Wycliffe, religious reformer, this created an unbridgeable chasm between lay people and their personal relationship with God, perpetuating the distance between the clergy and the people. He and his followers, known as the Lollards, set about translating the whole of scripture into English. It was a massive task, condemned as heretical, but thanks to the efforts of a network of sympathetic nobles, the English Bible spread across the country. In this way, as in many others, the Lollard movement was a Reformation before its time.

relationship of Church and State was instituted, eventually taking place under the protection of the Duke of Savoy in 1431. It came into conflict with the then pope, Eugene IV, over the old problems and ended with the Duke himself being elected as anti-pope. For all its original intentions, in the long run, the conciliar movement reinforced the claims of those who wanted a strong papacy.

The end of the medieval church

It is easy to look back on medieval churchmen and decide that they failed because they were corrupt. After all, even St Thomas Aquinas struggled with the problem of Christian poverty when so many of its exponents seemed to possess an excess of spiritual pride. Reforming popes believed it morally right that, as St Peter's heirs, they should direct secular governments towards the protection of the Church, both at times of military crisis and on a day-to-day institutional level. Medieval Europe was never a theocracy, but there were those who thought it should have been. Urban II and Innocent III came closest to being able to wield secular power as though it was their own – perhaps that was much of the point of the First and Fourth Crusades. But the Church was only one nation whose citizens permitted its leaders to rule, and it was a nation that sprawled over many others.

Wycliffe and Hus were the immediate forerunners of Protestantism, although the name had not then been claimed. Many of their teachings – criticism of the papacy, indulgences, monks, and bishops –

made sense to the wholly orthodox. Chaucer had mocked the parson in his *Canterbury Tales* in terms more comic but no less scathing than had Gregory VII scorned the illiterate priest, while humanist thinkers of the 12th and 13th centuries had explored the special relationship between the individual and God, and had found in it divine grace. Over the course of the Middle Ages, however, a growing religious literacy across Europe allowed such ideas to be extended to their logical conclusions. Wycliffe's precept "justification by faith", later Martin Luther's, might not seem so very radical, but it brought with it a rejection of all that was seen to be extraneous or diverting: confession and absolution before a priest, the intercession of saints, the penance of pilgrimage, and above all the authority of popes to bind and loose the sins of men either on earth or in heaven.

By the middle of the 16th century, Martin Luther had nailed 95 refutations of the practice of indulgences to a church door and Jean Calvin had denounced transubstantiation as "conjury". But if the tide was on the turn, it still had a long way to come in. Wycliffe had denounced what he called the magic of the medieval church, in particular exorcisms and hallowing, but we should not be too quick to bid medieval mysticism farewell. It is worth remembering that the sign of the cross, oaths on the Bible in court, faith healing, blessing with holy water and pilgrimage have all survived both the Reformation and the scientific revolution as parts of both Catholic and Protestant spirituality.

THE DAWN OF MODERN EUROPE

1400–1599

1400

1450

1493 Pope Alexander VI publishes a bull dividing the new world between Spain and Portugal.

1492 Subjugation of Granada. Ferdinand and Isabella end Moorish presence in Spanish peninsula and unite kingdoms of Castile and Aragon.

1485 Accession of Henry VII of England after the Battle of Bosworth ends the Wars of the Roses.

1477 Battle of Nancy. Defeat and death of Charles the Bold breaks power of Burgundy.

1431 Joan of Arc is executed by the English

1400   **1425**   **1450**   **1475**

1415 Jan Hus, Bohemian Protestant martyr burnt at the stake in Prague.

1450 Johannes Gutenberg develops moveable type for printing. The Gutenberg Bible, the first printed book, is printed in 1453.

1492 Columbus sets sail on *Santa Maria*. He arrives in the Bahamas in October.

1500

1524 Peasants Revolt in Germany.

1530 The Diet of Augsburg. Protestant movement in Germany takes institutional form.

1519 Election of Charles V as Holy Roman Emperor. Spanish conquistador Cortes completes his conquest of Mexico.

1533 Henry VIII is excommunicated by Pope Clement VIII. Henry becomes head of the newly formed Church of England in 1534.

1550

1571 Defeat of the Ottoman fleet at Lepanto by the Holy League of Spain, Venice, and Rome.

1572 St Bartholomew's Day Massacre. Over 3000 Huguenots die in Paris following the order of the massacre by Charles IX under the influence of his mother Catherine de'Medici.

1555 Peace of Augsburg brings settlement of religious question in Germany.

1598 Edict of Nantes brings end to religious war in France. Death of Philip II of Spain.

1568–1609 The Dutch revolt against Spanish rule in the Netherlands.

1587 Execution of the Catholic Mary Queen of Scots by Elizabeth I of England.

1558 Accession of Elizabeth I in England tilts strategic balance in Western Europe towards Protestantism.

1576 Sack of Antwerp by the Spanish.

1588 Defeat of the Spanish Armada by the English fleet.

---

0   **1525**   **1550**   **1575**   **1600**

1513 Machiavelli writes *The Prince* (published in 1532).

1508–20 Raphael is at work on the papal palace in Rome.

1516 Publication of Erasmus' *New Testament* and Thomas More's *Utopia*.

1517 Luther's protest against indulgences ignites the Reformation.

1519–21 Portuguese explorer Ferdinand Megallan starts his circumnavigation of the globe. In 1521 he reaches the East Indies (the Philippines) where he is killed. One ship returns to Spain to complete the circumnavigation of the globe.

1532–4 Publication of Rabelais' *Pantagruel* and *Gargantua*.

1532–43 Holbein is active at the court of Henry VIII.

1556 Ignatius Loyola dies. He was the founder of the Jesuit Order.

1568–80 Montaigne writes his *Essais,* which launch a new literary form.

1582 Italy, Spain, France, and Portugal adopt the Gregorian calender.

1594–6 Shakespeare writes first major plays for London theatre.

1599 Globe Theatre is built in London.

1547–64 Michelangelo paints the Sistine Chapel in the Vatican.

The spectacular victory of the Holy Alliance of Spain, Venice, and the pope over the Ottoman navy at the Battle of Lepanto in 1571 was a rare example of successful co-operation between European states against a common enemy. More often, competition would drive them into enmity and conflict with each other.

MODERN MONARCHIES AND STATES

At the dawn of the 16th century, the political map of modern Europe began to take shape. As the feudal regimes crumbled, a new administrative apparatus emerged as kingship became more confident and government more ambitious and wide-ranging than ever before.

The dawn of a new era brought important changes to the political map of Europe. France, a hundred years before, almost submerged beneath the challenge of England and Burgundy, emerged triumphant from the tribulation of the Hundred Years War. Suppression of the last independent apanages of Britanny and Bourbon early in the 16th century consolidated a rich and densely populated territory. Meanwhile, in the south, the unification of Castile and Aragon heralded the rise of Spain. When the Catholic monarchs, Ferdinand of Aragon and Isabella of Castile, applied the combined resources of their kingdoms to the subjugation of the Moorish kingdom of Granada in 1492, the last vestige of Muslim power in the peninsula was removed. At first the union of crowns was personal only, a consequence of their marriage: the full unification of the kingdoms was achieved only with the accession of their grandson, Charles of Ghent, also the heir to the rich Burgundian lands of the Netherlands. When, through his other grandfather Maximilian I, Charles was also able to make good his claim to the imperial crown in Germany, the Holy Roman Empire, a formidable new power, had emerged. Conflict with the other great continental power, France, was virtually assured.

Meanwhile, to the north and east, other new monarchies took shape. In England, the new Tudor dynasty emerged from the chaos of the Wars of the Roses eager to assert itself on the European stage. In Scandinavia, Sweden broke away from the Danish crown, to which it had been united for three centuries, beginning a bitter rivalry that would dominate the affairs of the Baltic for the rest of the century. All of these developments had two consequences of fundamental importance: the centre of gravity of European affairs moved north and westwards, and the moral ascendancy of the Italian city-states, during the medieval period both economic powerhouses and admired models of government, was effectively past.

The emergence of these new states had profound consequences for European society. Inveterate competitiveness bred a culture of display with rulers vying for the most sophisticated courts, the best music, and the most lively scholars and artists. This was Renaissance monarchy: costly, ostentatious, and elegant. The ambition to build territory brought a large increase of diplomatic activity as rulers sought to create alliances. Then, as states fell inevitably into war, the need to raise troops brought an increasing need for higher taxation.

As states were changing, so, too, was warfare. The growing effectiveness of firepower and artillery made the cavalry, the mainstay of medieval feudalism, far less potent. Instead, states raised ever larger armies of relatively untrained infantry. Sieges, rather than battles, increasingly defined the outcome of a conflict.

With the need for more taxes came the need for a more sophisticated feudal state to raise and spend the money. More and more, the crown aspired to direct rule over the furthest territories, rather than relying on the authority of the local magnate nobles as its representative. The institutional effect of these changes varied. In some parts of Europe representative assemblies became true partners in government, such as the Estates of Eastern Europe. Elsewhere, the king ruled through officials alone, and representative assemblies, such as the French Estates General, diminished in importance.

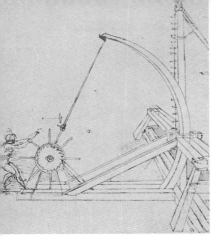

Science and Technology

The great advances of the 16th century would not have been possible without technical innovation, but most of the major technical advances were gradual and incremental, building on a body of knowledge inherited from the medieval period. Only with printing did the period witness genuine technological breakthrough.

Leonardo da Vinci, catapult – sketch. The technical advances of the Renaissance involved a restless quest for knowledge in all fields. In this respect, Leonardo da Vinci was the archetypal Renaissance polymath: a man for whom scientific observation and artistic endeavor were two sides of an all-encompassing search for new knowledge.

A page from the Gutenberg Bible. Printing represented the most staggering technical advance of the age, offering literally boundless growth in the capacities of the book to reach an ever expanding audience. Initially, however, purchasers still expected luxury artifacts, and many of the first books closely resemble the highly illustrated manuscripts they would gradually replace.

When it comes to the field of technological change it would be misleading to make too radical a distinction between the medieval world and the era that followed. Most of the truly transforming technological innovations arose out of the needs of medieval craft societies and through the patient application of trial and error. This was true both of printing – the triumph of medieval guild technology – and of the improvements in ship design that made possible long-distance voyages of discovery. Only new departures in the field of cartography illustrate a truly new world view at work, and here, ironically, the voyages of exploration were stimulated as much by the mapmakers' errors as by their successes.

Exploration

The voyages of discovery depended in almost equal degree on the new imaginative renderings of space created by cartographers. The seaman of the 15th century made more progress than the more scientifically inclined cartographers. In the world of cartography, much was made of the rediscovery of the work of the 2nd-century Greek mapmaker Ptolemy. From Ptolemy, Columbus and his contemporaries learned that the earth was a perfect sphere (an inaccurate observation, but universally believed at the time), and that the inhabited world extended in a continuous land mass from Europe to the easternmost limit of Asia. But the conclusions drawn from Ptolemy illustrate the dangers of this alluring but only partially accurate knowledge. If Ptolemy were right, sailing west across the ocean offered a plausible route to Asia's riches.

The spatial sense of the 15th century was only partially created from the visual images of maps. While Columbus revered Ptolemy, he was also inspired by prose classics that explored in more colourful ways the exotic glories of the East, such as the travels of Marco Polo and the fictitious work of John de Mandeville, a hugely popular travelogue later revealed as a complete fabrication.

Ignorance and misunderstanding thus played as critical a role in stimulating exploration as true knowledge and technological progress. The seafarers of the age built on far surer foundations with improvements in navigational techniques and ship design. By the 15th century, great strides had been made in the development of astronomical navigation. By the end of this century, the best Portuguese navigators could calculate their position at sea fairly accurately by a combination of observed latitude and dead reckoning.

The same process of trial and error brought notable steps forward in ship design and rigging. Following the introduction of the square-rigged sail on the main-mast in the 13th century, sailors gradually evolved the full-rigged ship of three masts. All of this innovation permitted a gradual increase in the size of vessels. At the beginning of the 14th century, the normal size of a Hanseatic ship was about 75 tons. By the 16th century, 400 tons had become a normal size for most cogs, and there were numerous Venetians carracks of 600–700 tons. Ships in Europe did not grow much above this size until after 1800.

Ptolemy's Map of the World. These rare, brilliant, and evocative cartographical creations illustrate the extent of the geographical knowledge of the ancients (reasonably accurate for Europe and the Levant), but also the frightening degree of ignorance of what lay beyond Europe.

Incremental change of the sort described here is impossible to identify with a particular date or period. The most dramatic technological change of the age – the invention of printing – can be far more accurately dated.

Advances in printing

Between 1440 and 1460, a small number of dedicated and inspired entrepreneurs tackled and solved the problem that unlocked the potential of the vast appetite for books which already existed in medieval society. The technical vision was in its day breathtaking, involving as it did the casting in metal of many thousands of individual letters of uniform size and style, to be used to ink an impression on paper or vellum (cured animal skin), before these could be dried, printed on the reverse, gathered, and folded to form a book. It was an extraordinarily complex, expensive, and daring endeavour, and it was the skills and technologies of the medieval guild society that made this possible, not least of which was the capitalization of such an ambitious project.

In the first years of printing, fortunes were lost amid acrimonious quarrels between inventor and investors. But the book soon outgrew its tentative beginnings and became an independent artefact in its own right. The first printed books appeared in Mainz, Germany, around 1455, yet within 30 years the new technology had been generalized around much of Western Europe. By 1480, printing had been established in at least 30 cities. By the first years of the 16th century, there were printing presses in over 100 locations, and certain European cities, such as Venice, Paris, Rome, and Antwerp, had already established reputations as major centres of book production.

By this time, the book, until recently the most experimental of technologies, was also attaining its mature form. In the larger, better financed houses, printers had successfully experimented with the use of more sophisticated specialized types such as Hebrew and Greek fonts. The initial slavish imitation of the appearance of manuscripts through a uniform body of text in one font size had given way to more ambitious compositions, using varying types, marginalia, decorative initial letters, and, in the most sophisticated books, woodcut text illustrations. As the publishing industry became established in this way, there sprung up around it a range of associated specialist trades: the bookbinders, type-founders, and merchants who specialized exclusively in the distribution and sale of books. The vastly increased demand for paper had spawned a huge increase in the number and quality of local paper mills. Most of all, printers had by now mastered the techniques for producing reliable texts at relatively modest prices, and this in turn had begun to transform the market for books. The age of mass literacy was now technically possible.

Cities and Education

Pre-modern society was rural and local. Ninety per cent of Europe's population lived in the countryside and depended on agriculture for its livelihood. Despite much patient attention to improving the productivity of their fields, agriculture remained overwhelmingly dependent on fickle circumstances outside human control: incidence of war, crop disease, and above all, the weather.

In the ceaseless search for improved farming methods, some progress was made in understanding the benefits of fertilization and the use of fallow crops such as turnips for crop rotation. But large improvements in crop yields remained in the future. That is not to deny that the rich could enjoy a wide and varied diet if they chose. Eager merchants would bring to the tables of noble households a vast variety of meat, fish, and game – though this did not necessarily make for variety of diet. Because they could afford it, many from society's higher echelons ate far too much meat and suffered in consequence agonies from ulcers and vitamin B deficiency. For those nearer the margins of subsistence, diet remained monotonous and low in quality. Bread, often made up of inferior grains and heavily adulterated, made up 80 per cent of the diet of the poor, eked out by milk and dairy products. In times of poor harvest, starvation loomed.

Such was life in the countryside, and it was no wonder that many from peasant families, particularly those who did not stand to inherit land, chose to make for the cities. But towns and cities could be perilous places. With so many people packed close together in unsanitary conditions, cities were busy, stinking places, with no source of clean water, and there was no real understanding of the need for efficient disposal of human waste. They could be deadly places: epidemic disease periodically ravaged their populations, and other natural disasters – fire and flood – were frequent visitors. In consequence, mortality was severe: no early modern cities could renew their population naturally and instead depended on steady inward migration to compensate for the high death rate.

Cities and trade

Nevertheless, people with ambition were increasingly prepared to take their chances in the cities, for these were the real motors of economic growth in pre-modern society. The large concentrations of people with disposable wealth created a ready market for luxury products, either home-made or imported. Cities were the crucial points in trade routes that, by the 16th century, stretched through the whole of Europe and beyond. The growth of international trade created its own specialized industries catering for the international market, such as banking and insurance. By the beginning of the 16th century, the established splendour of the Italian cities was rivalled by the new giants in northern Europe: Paris, Antwerp, Nuremberg, and Augsburg.

A view of Antwerp from the sea. This delicate, naturalistic view of northern Europe's rising entrepôt illustrates the importance of seaborne trade, much carried, as here, on tiny coasting vessels. Antwerp would enjoy a period of spectacular growth during this time as a centre of regional and international trade, before the vagaries of war brought decline.

Holbein's portrait of Erasmus

Scholar, philologist, political thinker, above all author and entrepreneur: Erasmus of Rotterdam was one of the most multi-faceted intellectuals of the 16th century and the first man ever to make a fortune from the craft of writing. His scholarly reputation was built on a seminal translation of the New Testament, and it was this that attracted both the admiration of Europe's scholars and the eager patronage of its crowned heads. Erasmus was not afraid to write also in a lighter vein, however, and it was these works, the *Adages*, satires, and correspondence, that made his fortune. Erasmus was courted by all who aspired to the company of scholars, including men such as the painter Hans Holbein, who created this delicate portrait.

For all that, economic growth depended on the established structures of medieval guild and trading societies. This was a craft-based rather than an industrial society. Indeed, the domination of the conservatively minded craft guilds, defending the rights and expertise of local masters, tended to militate against ambitious economic ventures. As a consequence, large-scale industrial enterprise tended to be concentrated in the countryside: this was true both of the established industries, such as coal- and silver-mining, and of newly developed techniques for the refining of iron and glass. Industries situated near towns were disadvantaged by the increasing scarcity of local supplies of wood or because their pollution of the city's water supplies aroused the ire of inhabitants.

Education and humanism

Cities were also major centres of information exchange and education. By the 15th century, almost all towns of any size had a Latin school, and many boasted a university. This was an age that witnessed a vast growth in demand for reading and writing skills among the laity, and a wish to free professional educational services from the traditional domination of the clergy. Later, in Protestant Europe, this movement received additional propulsion from the confiscation of Church property, although less of this was turned over to educational purposes than was originally intended. Throughout Europe, the new educational agenda was powerfully enhanced by the spreading influence of humanism.

Humanism was a multifaceted phenomenon: an intellectual movement, an aspiration of educational renewal, and, at a much more humdrum level, an educational curriculum. Taken at its most basic, humanism was the pursuit of a classical education, the study of the literature and languages of Ancient Greece and Rome. The study of the classics had a particular end in mind. Humanists were firmly convinced of the relevance of classical learning to modern life. The Renaissance desire to study classical languages and culture was partly aimed at recovering the achievements of that age. The core activity of the Renaissance scholar was the hunt for classical texts and, when they were discovered, the discernment of an authentic text by critical comparison of surviving manuscripts.

Humanism involved not only a new educational agenda, but also a new rhetoric. In an age that normally revered the past, humanism gloried in the denigration of earlier traditions of scholarship such as scholasticism. In bitter exchanges, the humanists would carry the day because their extraordinary self-confidence was combined with serious scholarly achievement. The rediscovery of classical texts and their diffusion in print led to the techniques of textual criticism that were among the enduring achievements of the Renaissance.

These achievements were personified by the career of Desiderius Erasmus. A scholar of unquestionable ability and a rampant self-publicist, he published work of enduring scholarly value, epitomized by his *Novum Instrumentum*, the groundbreaking translation of the New Testament from the original Greek. At the same time, through his more ephemeral satire and polemic, Erasmus came to personify the wider characteristics of humanism: arrogant, scathing, and unashamedly elitist. In the process, he was courted and idolized by Europe's rulers and made himself a fortune.

Exploration and Empires

The voyages of discovery paved the way for one of the most fundamental developments of world history: the domination of non-European cultures by the West. But the origins of this colonization lay in a mass of disparate and speculative ventures: perilous and foolhardy expeditions into the unknown by tough and reckless men.

This portrait of a Peruvian Indian, which exploits the Renaissance interest in the human form in a classic evocation of the "noble savage", demonstrates the collision of two conflicting visions of people who were the subject of both curiosity and suspicion.

Portugal and Spain led world exploration in the 16th century. Portuguese ships found routes through the Atlantic and Indian oceans to India. The Spanish headed westwards and discovered the Carribbean islands and the Americas. Magellan's

The eastern voyages

In opening up worlds beyond the Atlantic coasts, the peoples of Europe would owe an incalculable debt to the seafarers of Portugal. The Iberian kingdom, with its rugged extended coastline and lush coastal habitat, to a large extent already lived from the sea, and in the 15th century, the Portuguese had made steady progress in expanding the coastal and island regions known to Europeans. In 1415, a Portuguese army captured Ceuta in Morocco, and with this embarked on a progressive discovery of the West African coast. Ships driven off this coast chanced upon the important Atlantic islands, and these were progressively explored and colonized: Madeira, the Azores, and the Cape Verde Islands. By the 1460s, the Portuguese had reached the Gulf of Africa and Sierra Leone. As they pressed south, they learned that the Indian Ocean was accessible from the sea: a momentous discovery confirmed by the audacious voyage of Bartholomeu Dias, who in 1488 rounded the Cape of Good Hope. In the last years of the 15th century, Vasco da Gama at last confirmed the hope of this optimistic name by pressing on around the Cape to reach India. A decade later, the Portuguese were in China.

In 1519, the Portuguese explorer Ferdinand Magellan set off for what became the first circumnavigation of the globe. Having fallen from favour at the Portuguese court, he accepted a commission from Charles I of Spain to sail west to the spice islands of the Moluccas to ascertain that they were within Spanish territory. To reach his destination, Magellan navigated the southern tip of America and discovered the straits which bear his name. Returning, he took the unprecedented decision to head home by sailing westwards. Magellan was killed in 1521 in a battle with the natives of the Philippines. His journey was completed by his deputy, Sebastian del Cano.

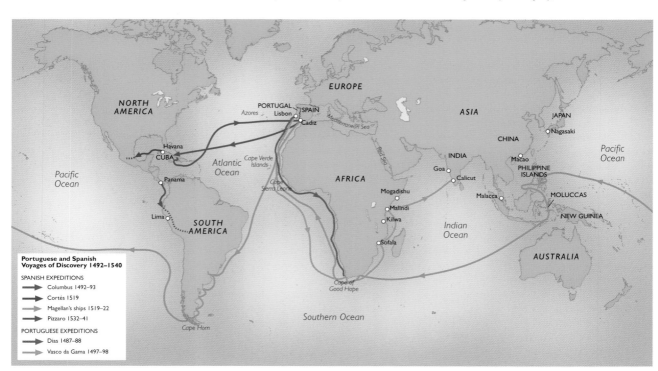

Portuguese and Spanish
Voyages of Discovery 1492–1540

SPANISH EXPEDITIONS
→ Columbus 1492–93
→ Cortés 1519
→ Magellan's ships 1519–22
→ Pizarro 1532–41

PORTUGUESE EXPEDITIONS
→ Dias 1487–88
→ Vasco da Gama 1497–98

The rapid and astonishing success of these voyages reveals the intelligent sense of direction and purpose that lay behind them. The major expeditions were sponsored by the crown; their clear and unclouded intention was to appropriate a large part of the rich Eastern trade. In the second decade of the 16th century, another brilliant seaman and royal servant, Afonso de Albuquerque, laid the basis of empire, taking Goa in India (1510), as well as the vital Malacca (1511) and Hormuz on the horn of Arabia (1515). These conquests set the tone for the Portuguese settlements, which would become a network of strategic trading ports, rather than colonies. The Portuguese had neither the men nor the resources to establish a colonial empire.

The western voyages

The character of the explorations to the East differed markedly from the rhythm of the westward enterprises. With voyages to the Indies, Europeans were dealing with familiar civilizations and known opportunities. The westward voyages were of an entirely different character. Here, what was to be experienced beyond the newly discovered Atlantic islands was a genuine mystery. The scanty scientific evidence available of this new world was simultaneously enticing and wholly misleading.

The motives of the first voyages mixed curiosity and greed in almost equal measure. But once the first conquistadors had subdued the rich indigenous civilizations, the gains to be had were all too obvious. In the 16th century, these went mainly to Spain, the first, and in this age the greatest, of the European imperial powers.

Colonization and exploitation

The cost to the indigenous peoples was very high. The campaigns of the first subjugation were swift and bloody, but it was the long process of exploitation that followed that took the greatest toll on lives. By the end of the century, the indigenous populations were devastated and the face of the continent changed for ever. Warfare, mistreatment, and harsh, unfamiliar labour all took a toll: most deadly of all were European diseases, against which native peoples had no immunity. The figures make terrible reading. The indigenous population of central Mexico, estimated at 25 million in 1521, fell to 16 million by 1532 and a pitiful 2.6 million in 1568. Comparable trends apply to many of the island settlements and the rest of Central America. In Peru, the decline was less severe, but still marked: from 3.3 million in 1520 to 1.3 million in 1570. In all regions, but particularly in the Caribbean islands, the maintenance of a functioning economy soon demanded large numbers of Africans as slave labour.

Even among these much reduced native populations, the new settlers were thinly spread. It is estimated that something short of a quarter of a million people of European origin emigrated to the Spanish New World dominions in the first 80 years after Columbus. In a survey of 1570, they represented little more than one per cent of the total population of the Spanish colonies. The new settlers were in the main landowners, engineers, and soldiers. From an early stage, too, missionaries were among their number, for the Spaniards proved almost as eager to save the souls of the indigenous populations as they were to exploit their wealth. In the first generation, the search for gold proved an unpredictable and frustrating business. But, from 1545, the Spaniards made a series of major strikes, all of silver: first at Potosí in Peru, then at Guanajuato and Pachuca in Mexico in the 1550s.

The Spanish silver mines soon came to have an almost mythical place in the European consciousness. The Spanish government developed an elaborate administration to protect the *Carrera de Indias*, a convoy system that linked Spain and the Indies. No wonder, for other European powers could not observe the extraordinary wealth that flowed from the Spanish and Portuguese overseas possessions without wishing to have their part.

The fabulous wealth revealed by the subjugation of the Aztec and Inca civilizations was a confirmation of hopes of wealth that fuelled the explorers' ardour from the time of the first voyages. In due course, plunder gave way to the search for new deposits; when the Spanish found silver, they opened up a new source of wealth that would shape European perceptions of the New World throughout the period.

Spanish Exploration

The new Spanish kingdom would be the principal beneficiary of the first great age of exploration. The bold incursions of the first explorers into unknown territory would create an empire of such wealth and grandeur that Europe's other powers feared the consequences for their own independence in the light of Spain's success.

Christopher Columbus's vision of westward expansion was built on a long history of frustrated initiative in many fields. As a seafarer, merchant, and keen but limited amateur cartographer, Columbus seemed destined to achieve little; however, it was the combination of these eclectic interests that allowed him to carry off his extraordinary and world-changing voyages.

The Inca Emperor Atahualpa as prisoner of the Spaniards at Cajamarca. The brutality with which the Spaniards dealt with their most illustrious captives demonstrated that the chivalric values which infused the knightly warrior code were not always adhered to in the new territories. Both Atahualpa and Montezuma were done to death after their safety had been assured.

Columbus

It was therefore something of an irony that the first significant force in Spanish voyaging was not Castilian, but the Genoese Christopher Columbus. Columbus's early career was that of many ambitious citizens of the Italian republics. What marked him out was a precocious interest in cartography and a determination to pursue exploration beyond the contours of the Atlantic islands. In other respects, Columbus would show the strengths and failings of his age. His appreciation of the world's continents was sketchy in the extreme, formed as much by fictional travel narratives as any exact knowledge. He also left something to be desired as a seaman: although he prided himself on his navigational skill, Columbus never mastered the art of measuring latitude. But he had discerned enough of the likely demand of long-distance ocean sailing to have the sense to re-rig the smallest vessel of his tiny first fleet, the *Niña*, from triangular lateen sails to a square rig. The little ship triumphantly stood the test of the voyage.

In August 1492, Columbus set sail from Palos with the *Pinta*, the *Niña*, and the *Santa Maria*. After 33 days of anxious sailing, land was sighted in the Bahamas. In three months of pleasant cruising round the islands, Columbus alighted on Hispaniola and, at last, found gold, before the loss of his flagship, the *Santa Maria*, necessitated a rapid return home.

On arrival in Spain, Columbus hastened to the royal court at Barcelona with natives and gold trinkets to convince his royal patrons that discoveries of significance had been made. In 1493, Columbus sailed again with a vastly larger fleet of 17 assorted caravels and pinnaces manned by some 1200 men. A swift voyage brought the fleet to San Domingo and thence to Hispaniola, where Columbus established a settlement, Isabella. Although Columbus was an explorer of genius and insight, as a colonial governor his skills never matched his gradiose ambitions. His new colony was poorly sited and badly led. By the time Columbus returned to Spain in 1496, it had effectively failed. Despite the fact that he had nothing to show for their sizeable investment in this second voyage, Columbus still had enough credit with the Spanish monarchs to win support for a new expedition in 1498, during which he discovered the vast continent of South America; however, the collapse of the colony of Hispaniola led to his removal and return to Spain in disgrace. A succession of tough-minded agents of the crown now began the settlement of the Caribbean islands in earnest. From these secure bases, other Spanish voyagers discovered and prospected the isthmus of Central America. In 1513, Vasco Núñez de Balboa led an expedition through the tropical forests of Panama to gaze, for the first time, on the Pacific.

The first encounter between Columbus and the Indians, as imagined by the 16th century Dutch painter and engraver Theodore De Bry. This image perfectly encapsulates the belief of the Europeans that they were bringing a superior way of life to heathen peoples. In a Biblical allusion, the Indians present Columbus with gifts of gold, frankincense, and myrrh.

The conquest of America

Of all the great histories of European expansion, nothing is as extraordinary as the destruction of the great empires of Mexico and South America. The Mexican empire of the Aztecs and the Inca dominion of Peru were two of the world's great civilizations, as even those who destroyed them recognized. From their base in the valley of Mexico, the Aztecs had, by 1500, created a well-settled dominion that stretched from the Pacific to the Caribbean. A population of around 20 million was divided between prosperous villages and great cities such as the capital Tenochtitlán (now Mexico City), a marvel that amazed all who saw it. Their carefully organized territories were unified by networks of roads and imperial institutions as sophisticated as anything then evident in Europe.

The conquest of the Aztec Empire was the work of Hernán Cortés, an experienced warrior who had made his reputation in the conquest of Cuba. His tiny force consisted of 11 ships, 600 men, and some 16 horses. Advancing into the interior, Cortés quickly grasped the Aztecs' unpopularity with their subject peoples, and hence their vulnerability. When Cortés completed the long march to Tenochtitlán, he acted decisively to seize the Aztec king, Montezuma and, through him, the city. This victory marked the end of the Aztec Empire.

Cortés was named as Governor General of the new territories, but a disastrous expedition into Honduras dissipated much of his political capital, and a commission of enquiry despatched from Spain threatened ruin. Although a personal appeal to the king initially rescued the situation, following the appointment of a new viceroy, Cortés abandoned his new lands to spend the rest of his days in Spain, having lost the favour of the court.

The conqueror of Mexico – Francisco Pizarro was the archetypal adventurer, an illegitimate, illiterate son of a soldier. Like Cortés, Pizarro had committed himself to the New World and by the time of his expedition to Peru, he was the veteran of several campaigns and had carved out a position of wealth and influence in the new town of Panama.

His expeditionary force was small: a mere 180 men and 27 horses. But his return to Peru coincided with the last stages of a debilitating civil war in the Inca kingdoms. Profiting from the confusion, Pizarro pressed inland to Cajamarca, where, under cover of a parlay, he treacherously captured the Inca king Atahualpa. Reinforced with a further 600 men, Pizarro was able to extract a huge ransom from Atahualpa, who was then put to death. The Inca army melted away, and the capital, Cuzco, surrendered. Peru was conquered, and Pizarro and his companions settled there to enjoy the spoils.

The real benefits, however, would be reaped by those who came after. The leaders of the Pizarro expedition almost all died violent deaths, as the greed and ambition that had fuelled their courage led to feuding. The consolidation of Spanish power required the presence of sober, experienced administrators: this was achieved with the establishment of viceroys in both Mexico (1535) and Peru (1543). Gradually the new men were able to impose a new sense of order on the conquered territories.

The Clash of Empires

As the full majesty of the Spanish discoveries became clear, Europe's other seafarers could not be expected to stand by idly. The assault on the Iberian monopoly of the New World began almost as soon as news of the discoveries began to circulate around the courts and seafaring communities of Europe. Despite this, Spanish power in the New World was not seriously threatened until the last quarter of the 16th century.

Spain and Portugal

In the first phase of maritime exploration, the dangerous potential clash between the kingdoms of Spain and Portugal was carefully avoided. Portugal had spurned Columbus's initial advances for patronage; however, a landfall at Lisbon on his return from his first voyage had alerted the shrewd Portuguese king to what might be accomplished by westward expansion.

With two major powers now strongly committed to exploration, the necessity of agreed lines of demarcation was apparent. The result was the Treaty of Tordesillas of 1494, agreed with the help of a complaisant Spanish pope, Alexander VI, and intended to separate a Portuguese zone of influence in Africa eastwards from the Spanish westward explorations. At the last moment, the Portuguese succeeded in pushing the line of demarcation 275 leagues westward, on the grounds that their ships were often forced to sail far out into the Atlantic to catch favourable winds for the southern voyage. Although they did not know it at the time, this would ultimately give them rights to the as yet undiscovered territories of Brazil.

France and England

In truth, Portugal was now fully occupied with the valuable Eastern spice trade and the less certain potential of Brazil. But other nations were quick to sense the profit in challenging the Spanish monopoly. As early as 1504, French privateers began raiding Spanish transatlantic shipping on the final stages of the voyage towards home waters. In 1523, one Jean Fleury even succeeded in detaching two vessels, bringing the wealth of the Mexican conquests back to Charles V. This spectacular treasure galvanized French seafarers into making a concerted assault on Spanish shipping, a campaign legitimized by the sporadic state of war between Emperor Charles V and the French king, Francis I. From the 1530s, the French corsairs extended their marauding into the Caribbean.

The French fared less well as colonists. Plans to settle in Brazil and Florida were easily repulsed by the Portuguese and Spanish, respectively. The collapse of these early colonizing ventures, and the subsequent preoccupation of the French Wars of Religion in the latter half of the century, left the way open for a new, and ultimately more formidable, interloper. English encroachment, always an irritant to the Spanish, grew ever more damaging, leading ultimately to a total rupture between the two nations. The English ventures flourished partly because the objectives of the voyages, left largely in the hands of hard-nosed seafaring captains, remained pragmatic and focussed on critical economic objectives. John Hawkins had visited the French colony at Florida only days before its final destruction, and he had seen the pitiful rabble to which it had been reduced. It was a hard lesson that small, undercapitalized colonial missions had little chance of success. Rather, the English would flourish by forcing an entry into the Spanish monopoly at its most vulnerable point – the lucrative trade in African

English colonists arrive at Roanoke Island, Virginia, first settled by Sir Walter Raleigh in 1585. The first Roanoke colony lasted a total of ten months. The colonists were ill prepared and were forced to rely on the local Indians for food.

The ships of the United East India Company arrive back in Amsterdam in 1604 after travelling to Indonesia to obtain spices. The United East Company could be considered the world's first modern company, with shares and shareholders, or subscribers.

slaves – and, as tension grew into open hostility, by blatant assaults on Spanish cargoes.

These expeditions, indignantly opposed by the Spanish authorities and surreptitiously financed by the English elite, gradually brought relations between the two powers to the point of collapse. But the English were less successful in this period as colonists. Even the charismatic leadership of Sir Walter Raleigh could not save the Virginian colony established on the river Roanoke. Determinedly and expensively reinforced from England, it enjoyed a fitful existence until 1590, when the latest fleet found the fort abandoned and the colonists disappeared. Raleigh returned to privateering; the Virginia colony was not revived until 1607.

The Dutch

The last decade of the century witnessed an intensification of the sea war and the first emergence of a power that would enjoy a great colonial future: the Dutch. The war against Spain had already taught the Dutch the profits to be made in preying on enemy shipping, and the emergence of a free northern state after 1585 set the Dutch on the road to more ambitious ventures. The final crucial element in this new venturing was the incorporation, since 1580, of the Portuguese crown in the dominions of the Spanish Philip II. In the short term, this made available to Philip the formidable Portuguese ocean-going fleet for his so-called "Enterprise of England". The damaging long-term consequence, however,

was that all Portuguese possessions had now become a legitimate target for the enemies of Spain.

The Dutch were not slow to take advantage. The great expansion of Dutch enterprise in the last years of the 16th century touched all aspects of Europe's most lucrative trading activities: the Baltic, Mediterranean, and Levant, the Africa trade, and the Caribbean. It was only in the final years of the century that the potential of the Indies trade was fully realized. At this point, in Amsterdam Dutch intervention came with the establishment of the "Compagnie van verre" (literally, the "Long Distance Company") by a consortium of nine rich businessmen. They pooled a capital of 290,000 guilders, enough to buy the equivalent of 60 or 70 large houses in Amsterdam. The fleet they sent out to the East Indies returned in 1597, and, although depleted and much diminished by the hardship of the voyage, the success of the venture ignited the imagination of the Dutch mercantile world. Other companies were founded to exploit the new opportunities, and, by the end of 1601, no fewer than 65 ships had sailed.

The danger of competition between rivals spoiling the trade spurred the states of Holland to step in. In 1602, after months of negotiations, the United East India Company was duly founded. By this time, too, the English had realized the promise of the East. The English version of the East India Company was first constituted, with a list of 101 subscribing merchants, in 1599. One of the great rivalries of the first imperial age was set to begin.

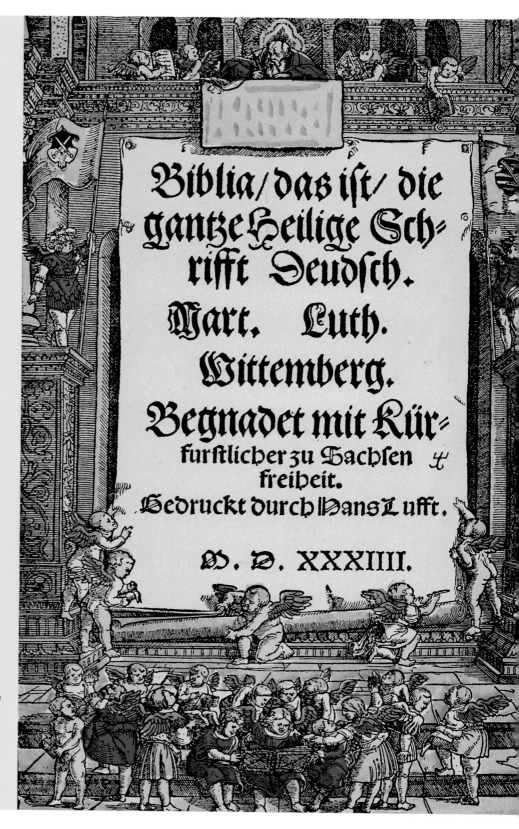

The title page of an early Wittenberg edition of Luther's German Bible. The German Bible was Luther's most enduring literary achievement, but for Protestantism it was only part of a torrent of print with which the evangelical leadership pressed its case. Luther wrote ceaselessly for an insatiable market; printers and publishers grew rich on the proceeds.

THE RISE OF PROTESTANTISM

Throughout the Middle Ages, calls for reform had been a constant part of the institutional life of the Church. It was not immediately clear why an obscure clerical quarrel emanating from Germany should pose so much more substantial a threat or why it should have created a movement – Protestantism – that permanently divided the Western Church.

In the last part of the 15th century, the Western Church seemed at last to have entered a period of calm after centuries of upheaval. The great and fundamental questions raised by the conciliar movement had finally been resolved, to the benefit of papal authority. After centuries in which prelates, scholars, and monarchs had disputed the claims of the papacy to theological authority within the Church, the popes had finally triumphed. The papacy was restored to Rome, and the dark days of the Schism, when rival popes ruled in Avignon, were banished for ever.

A series of dynamic patron popes threw themselves into re-modelling Rome as a capital fit for the Church and for the new age of the Renaissance. It was, ironically, an aspect of this rebuilding that would spark off what would become the Protestant Reformation. To finance the rebuilding of St Peter's Cathedral, Pope Julius II proclaimed a new indulgence: this device, already a major source of income for the late medieval Church, was to be exploited for a European fundraising effort. Indulgences were already controversial for reform-minded Catholics, as they coupled the suggestion of mercy in the afterlife with financial contributions: technically, they offered remission of pains in purgatory. But the pope, now Julius's successor Leo X, was clearly wholly unprepared for the storm that erupted when a previously obscure German friar, Martin Luther, spoke out against the fundraising campaign.

The initially laconic reaction to Luther in Rome is not surprising, but the challenge of Protestantism proved more threatening than medieval criticism for three main reasons. First, among the educated elite, the Church had to face the new challenge of humanism. In the first years, Luther's criticism struck a chord because, all over Europe, humanists had voiced similar concerns about clerical discipline, standards of education, and the abuse of papal power. Secondly, the humanist agenda coalesced with a more general sense of rising expectations among the laity, linked with a rise in literacy. They invested large amounts of money in the decoration of their churches and in employing more priests to say masses for their souls. Especially in Europe's confident urban communities, they expected high standards in return; where their clergy fell short, they gave Luther a hearing. Finally, the message of the reformers could reach a far wider audience than ever before through the recent invention of printing. This, most of all, explains why Luther's movement became an international one.

Building from their criticism of indulgences, Luther and his supporters would in due course pose a formidable challenge to Catholic orthodoxy. In the first years, most powerful – and most shocking – was the denunciation of the Church hierarchy. Once the papacy had failed to heed the call for reform, Luther was quick to identify it as the seat of the Antichrist; many would eventually accept his repudiation of papal authority without necessarily condoning the violence of his language. This courageous attack was fuelled by Luther's profound sense of calling. Here, Luther's theological basis was a reworking of the Augustinian doctrine of Grace that laid unusual stress on God's redemptive power, unassisted by the efforts of the individual fallen Christian (justification by faith). In the early years of the Reformation, this was all the more powerful because it was by no means clear to Catholics that this understanding of justification was heretical. By the time the Church had found its voice, the damage had already been done.

Martin Luther and John Calvin

In the early years of the German evangelical movement, Martin Luther was a towering presence: a personality of iron will and a preacher and writer of rare talent. His personality dominated the German reform movement. But it was left to others, notably the French lawyer John Calvin, to create the Church structures that would make Protestantism a permanent force in much of northern and western Europe.

This portrait of John Calvin captures well the steely restraint that contemporaries found so difficult to penetrate. A study in contrasts with the more gregarious and voluble Luther, the lawyerly Genevan helped to bring order and system to the Reformation after the first

Luther, Calvin, and their fellow reformers. This idealized portrait gallery was one of the most popular and widely reproduced images of the Bible. It provided an image of scholarly unity that was in marked contrast to the reality of bitter doctrinal disputes that divided many of those portrayed.

Martin Luther

Of all the provinces of the Western Church, the territories of the Holy Roman Empire, particularly the German core, were potentially the most troublesome for Rome. The rich city-states and rural territories (many ruled directly by their bishops) offered lucrative tax revenues and patronage, but Germans frequently expressed their frustrations at the lack of local accountability. These grievances were periodically presented to the imperial Diets – meetings of the princes and city representatives – as a formal catalogue or petition – *Gravamina*. The young Martin Luther was, however, an unlikely spokesman for this movement. From the time that he entered the Augustinian order, Luther achieved rapid promotion, then gained a Chair in Theology at the new university of Wittenberg. His career, until the indulgences con-

troversy of 1517, was a monument to what could be achieved within the Catholic Church. But Luther had also embarked on a theological journey, one that led to a fundamentally new understanding of the concept of Grace and salvation. Man, he believed, was saved by God's free gift alone, not by any works that man could perform during his life on earth. Initially orthodox, in the context of a debate over the fundamentals of papal authority, this would prove explosive.

Luther's criticisms of indulgences attracted immediate public interest. In April 1518, he attended a meeting of his own Augustinian order in Heidelberg and won many friends: to many, the early stages of the Reformation appeared a squabble between two religious orders, as the Dominicans supplied many of Luther's earliest opponents. Initially, the Church fought back by conventional means. Luther was sum-

moned to meet the papal legate in Germany, and only when he refused to submit were his views condemned, in the Papal Bull *Exsurge Domine* of 1520. Outraged, Luther denounced the papacy as the agency of the Devil and repudiated its authority. Now Luther argued that only Scripture could be the ultimate authority in a reformed Church. Luther was also shrewd enough to exploit the public sympathy for his treatment by adopting the larger criticisms of the clergy and Church affairs in Germany which touched the lives of the many thousands engaged by the indulgences controversy, but unable to understand the wider theological issues. The result, expressed in a torrent of pamphlets from Luther, was that Luther's cause and that of German reform became one. When the Emperor Charles V met Luther at the Diet of Worms to confirm the pope's condemnation in 1521, the order proved unenforceable. Within a few years, numerous German cities and territories had adopted the Reformation, and the Protestant movement was born.

Luther's movement did not carry all before it. Erasmus remained loyal to the pope, as did other notable figures such as the Frenchman Jacques Lefèvre d'Etaples, who criticized the Church, but believed that reform should come from within. Nearer to home, the German Peasants' War of 1524–5 showed the limits of the social and political aspirations that could be accommodated within Luther's magisterial reform. The peasants saw Luther's attack on the Church as proof of divine support for their economic grievances, but Luther condemned the revolt, which added to its defeat. After the slaughter of the peasant armies, the remnant of the movement drifted into the radical fringes of Anabaptism, denounced by Luther. The Anabaptist movement reached its climax with the seizure of the north German city of Münster in 1534. Proclaimed the New Jerusalem in anticipation of the imminent end of time, Münster and its experimental Anabaptist government attracted many thousands of followers from all over northern Europe, before the increasingly erratic behaviour of its self-styled king, John of Leiden, brought the whole experiment into disrepute. Münster was put down with great ferocity in 1535, but the movement lived on, always on the fringes of society, but tenacious and brave.

The extremes of Münster were a propaganda gift for Catholic critics of the Reformation and effectively destroyed the early hopes of consensual evangelical renewal. Most damaging of all in this regard was the quarrel between Luther and Huldreich Zwingli, the leader of the Reformation in the Swiss Confederation. Zwingli, originally an admirer of Luther, had orchestrated the conversion of Zurich, the largest of the Swiss city-states, at an early date. But he nurtured an

The Reformation Broadsheet
This famous image was one of the most widely circulated of the polemical images of the Reformation. It skilfully combines the burning issue of the first years of the conflict (Luther's protest against indulgences) with his fierce denunciation of papal power: here the pope is identified with the seven-headed dragon of the Apocalypse. Such images were widely disseminated in the first decades of the evangelical protest and did much to build identification with the evangelical cause.

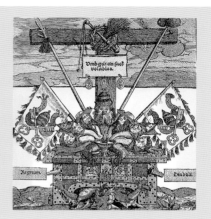

interpretation of the reform agenda more radical in several respects, practical and doctrinal, than Luther would allow. Luther was repelled by the visual austerity of Zurich worship, where in contrast to Wittenberg all images and statues had been removed as unacceptable. He also found Zwingli's austere Eucharistic theology unpalatable. The two men were tempted to express their differences in print, and a damaging pamphlet war ensued. An attempt to reconcile the two leaders at the Colloquy of Marburg in 1529 achieved nothing, and, when Zwingli was killed two years later leading Zurich's troops against the armies of the Catholic cantons of the Confederation, Luther could not disguise his satisfaction.

For a decade or more, the two Reformations went their separate ways. The initial rapid progress of the movement flagged. Although in Germany the work of church-building continued, in France, the Netherlands, and elsewhere, official repression stifled the initially vibrant evangelical movements.

John Calvin
The Reformation needed a second wind, and it found it through the work of the French evangelical John Calvin. A fugitive from the clampdown on evangelicals in Paris in the mid-1530s, Calvin found a new home in the small French-speaking city of Geneva, on the periphery of the Swiss Confederation. Under his tutelage, Geneva was transformed into a model of the Reformed Christian community. Meanwhile Calvin articulated, most notably in his *Institutes of the Christian Religion* of 1536, the systematic theology that the movement had thus far lacked. Calvin's system was remarkable both for its clarity and its comprehensiveness, drawing on the best of both the German and Swiss theological traditions in a masterful evocation of the new Christian vision of God, the Church, and society. It was the secure rock on which to build the second great age of Protestant expansion.

Henry VIII and Elizabeth I

At the beginning of the 16th century, England lay at the very periphery of European affairs. A century later, its position had been transformed, through the kingship of the Tudor dynasty: the emerging kingdom was now the lynchpin of European diplomacy. Presiding over this English Renaissance were two outstanding monarchs: the monstrous egomaniac Henry VIII and his wilful, enigmatic daughter, Elizabeth I.

The accession of the Tudor dynasty in 1485 followed a period of profound instability in English affairs. The Wars of the Roses (1450–85) had seen the crown of England change hands seven times over the course of 40 years of brutal fighting among nobles. The fortuitous triumph of Henry Tudor, the distant Welsh heir to the Lancastrian claim, was only possible because of the elimination of so many other leading figures. But the new king, Henry VII, showed an instinct for rule that made light of his previous inexperience. Former Yorkist opponents were either pacified or cowed into obedience, and the depleted royal finances restored through capable husbandry. The birth of two sons, Arthur and Henry, raised the prospect of the peaceful, uncontested succession for which all of England yearned. When the much-loved Arthur died prematurely in 1502, it was Henry who stepped forwards to claim the kingdom on his father's death in 1509.

The young Henry VIII was all that Europe expected in a king. Tall, handsome, and vigorous, Henry combined the traditional passions of the aristocracy with the new cultivated tastes of the Renaissance monarch. His passion for jousting and sports existed alongside more cultivated tastes, such as music and literature.

Henry planned to build on his father's achievement by ensuring that England was respected on the international stage. He quickly plunged the nation into the complexities of European affairs. By 1511, English armies were in France; a poor performance there was compensated by the crushing victory over the Scots at Flodden in 1513. The young king's enthusiastic war-making at least forced Europe's rulers to court him as an ally. Through the 1520s, an English alliance was pursued by both the Emperor Charles V and King Francis I of France. But as the years wore on, the diplomatic round took on a greater urgency. By 1529, it was clear that Henry's wife, Catherine of Aragon, would not bear him a son. A divorce was necessary, but the pope, among other reasons much indebted to the emperor

(Catherine's nephew), could not oblige. Failure to solve this diplomatic conundrum brought disgrace to Henry's faithful minister, Cardinal Wolsey, the architect of his military campaigns. Now, new men emerged to propose more radical solutions to "the King's Great Matter".

The opulence and pomp of this formal portrait of Henry VIII by Hans Holbein does not disguise the iron will of a man determined that his word would be law. By turn capricious and brutal, cultured, and intelligent, Henry was by and large admired by subjects desperate for security after decades of dynastic insecurity.

In 1532, the frustrated king took a new love, Ann Boleyn, and a solution could not be long delayed. Henry repudiated both his wife and the authority of the pope. An obedient Parliament enacted legislation that both confirmed English independence from Rome and established the king's royal supremacy over the Church. This was not Protestantism – Henry never shifted from the theological orthodoxy of his youth – and those Protestants who moved too fast did so at their peril. But in practical terms the changes introduced in Henry's new Church differed little from the reforms of continental Protestant princes. By 1540, England had a vernacular Bible, and Parliament had abolished purgatory, shrines, and pilgrimages. Most important, the dissolution of the monasteries had stripped the Church of much of its land and one of its most important institutions.

The crisis of mid-century

Henry's death in 1547 ushered in difficult years. Only Henry's third wife, Jane Seymour, had borne Henry the long-wished-for son, who now succeeded as Edward VI at the age of nine. His youth demanded a minority administration: power was exercised by his maternal uncle, the Duke of Somerset. Somerset was removed by his fellow councillors in 1549, but the new chief minister, the Duke of Northumberland, continued his policies, and, by 1553, England had a full Protestant Church settlement. When Edward died in 1553, on the verge of active kingship, all of this was thrown into question. The rightful queen, Mary, the daughter of Catherine of Aragon, was a firm Catholic, and the failed attempt to divert the succession to Lady Jane Grey only confirmed her determination to reintroduce the Catholic faith. Marriage to Philip of Spain (later Philip II) further cemented this decisive reorientation of policy.

But Mary, too, was destined for disappointment. The marriage with Philip drew England inexorably into Spain's quarrels abroad, but did not produce the heir that would have secured the Catholic succession. So when Mary died in 1558, childless and disappointed, the bruised kingdom fell to Elizabeth, the last of Henry's children and the last hope of the Tudor line.

The Elizabethan age

The new queen acted quickly to reverse both the Spanish friendship and her sister's religious priorities. A new Church settlement established Protestantism once and for all as the religion of England. Although Protestants schooled in the continental Churches of Geneva and Germany would regret that Elizabeth would not adopt their precepts in all things, this new Anglican Church still firmly aligned England with Europe's Protestant powers.

Puritan criticism of Elizabeth's Church grew gradually less strident as the reign wore on. By the last critical decade, all but a few unreconciled separatists identified strongly with the new Protestant state.

Abroad, England emerged as the most formidable opponent of Spanish power. The voyages of Hawkins, Drake, and Raleigh exposed the vulnerability of the Spanish Empire, and England's help to Protestant rebels abroad finally provoked Philip II beyond endurance. When the Spanish Armada set sail in 1588, the peril was great – English armies were inexperienced and unprepared, and only the Channel stood in the way of Philip's invading army. Elizabeth's luck held, however, and the destruction of the Spanish fleet tipped the balance of the conflict decisively in England's favour.

At home, too, this was a period of great achievement. Elizabeth was blessed with a generation of fine ministers, and the frequent meetings of Parliament to raise taxes and enact religious change had confirmed its role in the government of the kingdom. Most of all, this was a golden age for English culture. The work of Shakespeare and his contemporaries transformed English literature and enabled the English language finally to shed its dependency on more confident continental cultures. When Elizabeth died in 1603, England was poised for its emergence as one of Europe's greatest powers.

After years of a relatively weak and uncertain role, Elizabeth I helped restore the prestige of the failing house of Tudor by recreating the strong imperial kingship of her father. Portraits of the Virgin Queen were widely circulated among noble and gentry households as a tangible symbol of allegiance.

The Battle of Mohàcs, 1526. The
most decisive battle of
the 16th century decimated the
Hungarian nobility, extinguished
the Jagiello dynasty, and left
central Europe exposed to Turkish
conquest. Only the Habsburgs
could successfully fill such a void.

THE CHALLENGE OF THE EAST

In the 16th century, many of Europe's rising nation-states, and most notable events, were congregated on its Atlantic fringe. But no one underestimated the importance of events further east: the growing Habsburg Empire and the looming power of the Ottoman Turks.

One of the most significant, if hardly known, battles of the 16th century took place on the plains of Hungary near the town of Mohács, on 29 August 1526. On this fateful day, the young King of Hungary, Louis Jagiello, led his army against the Ottoman host. By nightfall, the Hungarian army was shattered: the king and the cream of his nobility lay dead on the battlefield.

With the death of King Louis, the Jagiello dynasty was extinguished, and a dangerous power vacuum opened up in one of Europe's most critical regions. Fifteenth-century Bohemia was one of the richest and most prized kingdoms of the growing Holy Roman Empire. Both Hungary and Bohemia were closely connected with the economic and cultural life of Germany, as, to a lesser extent, was Poland to the north. In all of these lands, humanism and the Renaissance had made a deep impact, leaving behind a fine legacy of scholarship, libraries, and buildings.

These, then, were the proud and rich cultures that seemed in 1526 to lie prostrate before the Ottoman advance. The thankless task of defending Christendom's vulnerable eastern flank fell to Ferdinand of Habsburg, brother of Emperor Charles V. Ferdinand exploited the marriage connection between the Habsburg and Jagiello dynasties to claim the Hungarian throne – but a portion of the Hungarian nobility preferred the local magnate John Zápolya, and a damaging civil war threatened to undermine the necessary defensive conflict against the Ottomans.

Gradually, Ferdinand asserted his authority and stabilized the front. The Habsburg presence in Eastern Europe, established in these unpropitious circumstances, would become a permanent feature on the European political landscape. Thus was born the Austro-Hungarian Empire – one of Europe's most enduring, if troubled, great powers.

The confrontation of the Habsburg and Ottoman empires was one of Eastern Europe's most significant geopolitical conflicts; the other was the struggle for supremacy in the Baltic. In the far north lay Denmark and Sweden, until the early years of the 16th century part of the united kingdom of Scandinavia. In 1521, Sweden claimed independence, but bitterness lingered between the two, to be reignited later in the century in the Great Northern War. These quarrels inevitably drew in Poland, the great sprawling kingdom along the southern Baltic shore. Poland-Lithuania played an important part in the politics of the era, both through its strategic location and through a growing reputation as a haven of toleration for refugees from the period's religious conflicts. In the second half of the 16th century, Poland was a multi-confessional state, presided over by benign monarchs and an enlightened nobility. In the last decades, the failure of the Jagiello dynasty brought difficulties, particularly as the Polish tradition of elective monarchy offered little continuity, and those elected often proved shallow in their commitment to Polish interests. The eventual victory in this contest of the Swedish Vasas dragged Poland inexorably into Scandinavian quarrels.

Looming further to the east was the vast brooding power of Muscovy. For much of the century, during the long minority of Tsar Ivan, Muscovy was consumed by internal troubles, but as Ivan grew to maturity the sleeping giant stirred. In the late 16th century, Ivan – aptly named the Terrible – was a turbulent and malign presence in European politics. He returned to haunt the Poles at frequent intervals, proposing himself as king when the crown fell vacant in 1572 and taking advantage of Poland's internal preoccupations to pounce on Livonia in 1558 to increase access to the Baltic. Many breathed a sigh of relief when, on 18 March 1584 and exactly as predicted by his 60 astrologers, Ivan suddenly expired.

The Ottoman Empire

The Ottoman advance through Europe struck terror through the hearts of Europe's citizens. As the Turks continued their march through the remnant of Byzantium, few could perceive that Western Christendom was encountering a rich and subtle civilization, and one from which European society had much to learn.

A miniature showing the parade of the Ottoman army before the walls of Tiflis after the fall of the city during the Ottoman war against the Persians. The soldiers recruited among the subject European peoples of the Balkans played an essential role in the Ottoman expansion eastward.

The Ottoman threat

By the end of the 15th century, a considerable portion of the European land mass lay in Turkish hands. The fall of Constantinople in 1453 falls near the mid point of the two centuries of steady Ottoman progress through the Balkans towards Latin Europe. In the hundred years before they took Constantinople, the Ottomans had already invested and colonized much of the Byzantine hinterland, including Thrace, Bulgaria, and Macedonia. Two campaigns in 1454 and 1455 smashed the Serbs, in territorial terms the largest geographical buffer between the Ottoman Empire and the West; the fall of Nova Brno also gave them control of its important silver and gold mines.

In the following decade, the Turkish advance enveloped the rest of the Greek peninsula (1458–61), followed by Herzegovina (absorbed 1483) and Albania (1468–78). Meanwhile, Venice was progressively driven back in the struggle for the Aegean Islands and the Dalmatian (Adriatic) coast. In 1520, the Ottoman host seized Belgrade, the southern key to Hungary; the triumph of Mohács then allowed the progressive occupation of much of Hungary. In 1529, they advanced to threaten Vienna: Western Europe lay open, and apparently defenceless before their conquering army.

The Ottoman advance towards the heart of Christian Europe, and particularly the collapse of the kingdom of Hungary, had a profound impact on the European psyche. For Martin Luther in Wittenberg, not so very far away, the victory of the Turkish horde was a sure sign of the imminent end of time. Several times during his career he had addressed the issue of the infidel threat to Christian society, and even as his life drew to an end he still gave anxious thought to the Turkish advance. In 1541 the final assault on Buda prompted him to publish an *Admonition to Prayer* against the Turks, in which he explicitly interpreted the present peril as a judgement on the German people for their sins. Two years later, in 1543, he wrote to the Saxon elector declining a personal exemption from the Turkish war tax. "I want," he declared, "to fight the Turk with my poor man's penny, alongside the next fellow; and who knows whether my little free-will offering, like the widow's mite, may not do more than all the rich compulsory taxes."

Luther died before the Ottoman advance into Europe had reached its high tide. Moldova was subsumed into Turkish territories in 1538, and later raids brought chaos and panic to both Transylvania and the borderlands of Polish territory. It would be many years before the inhabitants of central Europe would be able to feel secure in their future. In the meantime large numbers of Europe's former Christian peoples were forced to accommodate themselves to the reality of Ottoman rule.

By 1500, the Ottoman Empire covered the lands to the south and west of the Black Sea. As the century progressed, the Ottomans focused on Europe, advancing first into Moldavia, then Hungary after the Battle of Mohács in 1526. Their unsuccessful attempt to lay siege to Vienna in 1529 marked the limit of their progression west, but they continued to apply pressure to the border of the Habsburg Empire for the rest of the century.

Majolica charger showing Eastern horseman

Fascination with the Eastern civilizations was by no means confined to those who lived directly along the threatened borders. News of the Turkish wars provided healthy profits for enterprising publishers in all of Western Europe, often in little books of two or more sheets that drew on a small array of stock illustrations and formed part of the popular sensation literature of the day. Such tales did little to build real knowledge of Ottoman civilization, but among Europe's elites there was a growing recognition of the qualities of a civilization that was more than merely a potent military power.

Life under Ottoman rule

For all the scholarly writings and pamphlets devoted to the Turkish threat, one senses that the Western European public actually knew very little of life under Turkish rule. In particular, they had little sense of what Ottoman rule must have meant for the approximately 5 million Christian peoples settled in the Turkish provinces within Europe. Fed a diet that repeatedly harked on the ruthless cruelty of the sultan and the pitiless ferocity of his soldiery, the realities of the situation might well have surprised them.

The Ottomans, for instance, never attempted any forced or large-scale Islamicization of the Balkans. To exploit the new lands, they continued most of the existing tax regime, overlaid with their own new system for the extraction of a steady tribute from agricultural areas. Certain local taxes and dues were reserved for the sultan, others allocated to support the local administration of the appointed Turkish officials. The cornerstone of Ottoman rural administration was the *tinar* system – grants of rights of exploitation to selected *sipalvi*, originally trusted servants who had played their part in the conquest. Revenue was raised through a modest levy of peasant labour service (three days a year, much as had been customary under Christian rule) and a more substantial tithe on the annual harvest.

The Ottoman system also relied heavily on these captured Christian provinces for providing recruits to man their armies, which could then be deployed to face Muslim rivals in Anatolia (southern Turkey) and the Arab world. Most famous and notorious amongst these recruits were the janissaries: Christian children forcibly removed from their homes to be brought up to serve the sultan. The youths were given new Muslim names and obliged to adopt the Islamic faith; those who refused faced death.

The human suffering that underpinned such a system is obvious, but for those who managed to come through the strict training, the life of a janissary offered considerable career opportunities. A substantial number from the ethnic subject peoples in due course rose to become some of the most privileged and powerful soldier administrators in the Ottoman Empire. Of the 49 grand vezirs who served the sultan between 1453 and 1623, a clear majority was of Christian European origin, including at least 11 Slavs, 11 Albanians, and six Greeks; only five were of Turkish extraction. The Balkan peoples were an essential agent of the expansion of Ottoman influence throughout the Arab world.

The conquerors also made no attempt to suppress the Eastern Orthodox Church. On the fall of Constantinople in 1453 the Sultan personally selected a new Patriarch. His choice, a popular monk named Gennadius, was significant, since the Sultan chose a man who had led opposition to a possible reunification of the Catholic and Orthodox churches proposed at the Council of Florence in 1439. The Turk thus offered a broad hint that conditions under Ottoman rule might be preferable to the patronising and unfavourable conditions offered by Rome. And indeed, for most Orthodox Christians, life under Ottoman rule was not oppressive. The Church retained extensive jurisdiction in civil and family matters such as marriage and inheritance, where Ottoman law was not easily applicable. In return, the local clergy took a conspicuous role in local administration, even acting as assessors and collectors for taxes levied by the Ottoman state apparatus. The role of the Orthodox clerics in the Turkish structure of administration did not always increase their popularity with the subject peoples of the Balkans. By some, the clergy were regarded as little more than

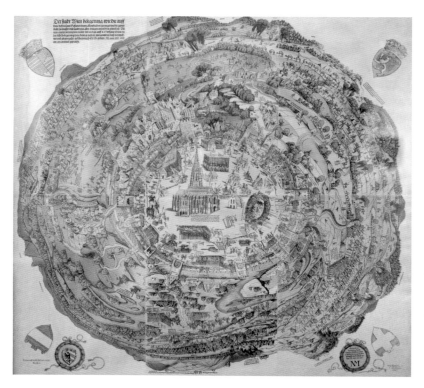

A circular map depicting The Seige of Vienna in 1529. The Ottoman Turks encircled Vienna, inflicted severe damage on her suburbs and on the surrounding vineyards, but withdrew after only 25 days.

collaborators. The first century of Ottoman rule brought a progressive drift of the Christian population from town to countryside, as the towns became ever more prominent as centres of Ottoman influence. The absence of vitality in the towns was one reason why the Eastern part of Europe did not share in the rapid improvement of educational standards among the peoples of western Europe. But the Orthodox church also played its part in retarding technological progress: fiercely conservative, it set its face against the march of science. It was this cultural separation, rather than conscious policy on the part of the region's Ottoman rulers, that lay behind the progressive distance that grew up between the Balkan lands and the rest of Europe.

Turning the tide

With the slowing of the Turkish march through Eastern Europe in the middle decades of the century, attention gradually switched to the Mediterranean. From the middle of the century this became the critical theatre, and the fulcrum of Christian fears. In 1534 the corsair Barbarossa had raided southern Italy, and then occupied Tunis. Since he already ruled Algiers, the threat to Christian shipping in the Western Mediterranean was all too obvious. But in 1541 an attempt by the Emperor Charles V to wrest control of Algiers was a costly failure. The Christian fleet was forced to withdraw with over 4000 casualties. It

would be left to Charles V's son Philip II to take up the challenge, and attempt to define a limit to the expansion of Turkish power in Southern Europe.

Philip did not underestimate the size of the task. A first attempt to confront the problem of Ottoman power in Western Europe, the Djerba expedition of 1559, was an unmitigated disaster. The swift arrival of the Turkish fleet led to an undignified retreat, leaving 10,000 Spanish captives to be paraded in triumph through the streets of Constantinople. It was Suleiman's attempt to push home this advantage, with an attack on the strategic island of Malta, that gave the first indication of a change of fortunes. Malta held out through an epic siege, and its relief by a Spanish fleet from Naples was celebrated throughout Christian Europe. It required years of patient diplomacy before Philip could create a diplomatic alliance capable of carrying the battle into the Turkish heartland; but by 1571 a Christian fleet was ready to do battle. The victory at Lepanto was one of the most spectacular in the history of naval conflict. The Turks lost 30,000 men and all but 30 of their 230 ships; the losses to the Holy League were only ten of their galleys.

The victory of Lepanto was a massive psychological fillip to Christian Europe, and especially to the architect of the Holy League, Philip of Spain. Strategically it achieved less than had at first seemed likely. The Turkish Empire worked feverishly to create a new fleet, and in 1574 this new force recaptured Tunis. The Holy League had already fallen prey to its internal rivalries; in 1573 Venice had established a separate peace. But if soaring Christian hopes had quickly to be scaled back, the decisive campaign in the eastern Mediterranean did at least establish a sort of equilibrium. By the end of the decade, Spain and the Turkish Empire had established a cautious truce; both their priorities had in any case shifted elsewhere. East and West were now able to contemplate a tentative relationship between two contrasting societies without the imminent fear of being overrun.

Two civilizations

What then can be said, in summary, of the impact of the Ottoman Empire in Europe? Certainly there was a certain curiosity about Arabic culture, shared by even so trenchant a critic as Luther. In 1537, he published with a new preface an edition of a 15th-century account of captivity under the Ottomans. Five years later, he published a free translation of the exposition on the Koran by the 13th-century Dominican Ricoldus, an indication of a growing interest in the languages and customs of the East that became increasingly a feature of erudite western circles.

This interest in the positive aspects of Eastern culture was one side of a complex relationship. The

An engraving of the Ottoman forces preparing for the siege of Vienna. Images such as this, depicting the Turks' exotic outfits and ferocity in battle, played a part in creating and perpetuating the view of these people as alien and cruel.

hardening of fronts in the second half of the century did not diminish fear of the Turk as an alien and deeply threatening force. Many European printers, in France, Germany, Italy and the Netherlands, made a steady living with news from Europe's Eastern borders. Through the second half of the 16th century the Lyon publisher Benoist Rigaud turned out scores of small pamphlets, recording the latest sensations from the war front: the battles, campaigns, escapes and atrocities. For these books he procured a small stock of woodcuts featuring figures in oriental dress and frenetic battle scenes, which he cannily re-used for numerous different books. Literature for the mass market in this way peddled a repetitive range of limited stereotypes, especially the cruelty, implacability and strangeness of Turkish mores.

Such books fed one particular view of the Ottoman menace; but there was another, more reflective perception which gradually came to play its part in western culture. For more discerning readers, the publishers of Europe offered a quite different tradition of literature that reflects a real fascination with an ancient and advanced civilization: its customs, social institutions, and political structures. Many of these books were lavishly illustrated with woodcuts of the costumes, plant life and topography of the East.

To feed this hunger for knowledge western readers were deeply indebted to the small number of people who travelled to the heart of the Ottoman Empire. Most were merchant traders, or diplomats who went by sea straight to the great city of Constantinople. Others, more intrepid, took the landward route through the Balkans, visiting a sequence of cities (such as Esztergom, Belgrade and Sofia) progressively more touched by their new masters. Such travellers were struck almost equally by the residual elements of western civilization and style (particularly remains from the Roman Empire) as by signs of Ottomanization, most notably the prominent minarets of the newly built mosques. Travellers also had strategic questions. They wanted in particular to understand why the Ottomans were so successful in military terms, and why so much Christian territory had been lost.

In this last question lies the key to why, in an age where cultural difference was more often despised than applauded, the Ottoman Empire was accorded a more than grudging respect. It was only in later centuries that travellers would be struck less by the exoticism of Balkan and Ottoman society than by its "backwardness". These later authors clearly regarded the Balkans as part of the Orient, and identified everything unsavoury they observed – poverty, dirt and disorder – as an aspect of the Ottoman system.

But the transition from the great apocalyptic threat to Christian civilization perceived by Luther, to the "Sick Man of Europe", lay far in the future. The best that can be said for the 16th century is that once the first tide of eschatological fear had receded, there were many in Western Europe who were prepared to recognize the Ottoman Empire for what it certainly was: an ordered society and a great civilization, worthy of study.

Sala del Capitolo of the Scuola Grande di St Rocco in Venice. Decorated by Tintoretto, the opulent magnificence of this Baroque chamber demonstrates the growing self-confidence of a Catholic culture gradually emerging from the shadow of relentless Protestant criticism.

THE COUNTER-REFORMATION

In the longer term, the rise of Protestantism would stimulate Europe's Catholics to undertake a wholesale re-evaluation of their beliefs and practice. But that, inevitably, took time: in the first critical decades, the most effective defenders of the old faith would be rulers of a traditional cast of mind, men like Emperor Charles V and Philip II of Spain.

The growth of Protestantism presented the Catholic Church with some difficult problems. Although Rome was quick to condemn Luther's heresies, many within the Old Church acknowledged that his beliefs were built on a sound tradition of Catholic teaching – it could hardly be otherwise, given his background and training. Reform-minded Catholics could also hardly deny the urgency of reform, and many shared his low estimation of the capacity of the popes to provide the impetus.

The first two decades after the beginnings of the German Reformation were exceptionally difficult times for Catholicism. From the first days, the teachings of Luther and his allies were vehemently opposed by those who recognized early on the full implications of his rejection of papal authority. Most of all, it remained uncertain precisely what was being defended. In France, the question of how far Catholicism could accommodate reform – and what reform – was hotly debated for more than two decades. In Germany, conferences between Protestants and Catholics aimed at the reconciliation of theological differences continued with some hopes of success until the Colloquy of Regensburg in 1541. Even after this, powerful forces within the Catholic establishment in Italy continued to explore theological formulations that were by no means incompatible with the Protestant understanding of justification by faith. When this failed, there were further high-profile defections to Protestantism.

In these circumstances, with the Church itself so uncertain, in the first half of the 16th century the more effective defence of Catholicism thus came from those who had been the leading stakeholders in the pre-Reformation Church: Europe's Catholic rulers. There was enough resistance among them to ensure that the Reformation outside Germany would suffer some notable reverses. Francis I punctured the optimism of those who hoped for reform in France through the executions of Louis de Berquin in 1529 and Etienne Dolet in 1546. However, the defence of the faith by these methods had distinct limitations. The Church was always vulnerable to a personal volte-face by the monarch, or a change of ruler. The same Henry VIII who burned the Protestants John Lambert and Robert Barnes also decided that theological conservatism could be consistent with repudiation of the pope.

It was for these reasons that the defence of the old faith became so closely associated with the personal crusade of the Habsburgs. There was never a real chance that the young Emperor Charles V would tolerate Protestantism. Although he was brought up at the sophisticated Burgundian Court, his personal faith had more in common with the Spanish core of his dominions. Here, the Catholic Church was perceived in a more positive light, respected and revered for its part in the reconquest of the Spanish peninsula. Charles manifested a similarly straightforward allegiance to the faith of his fathers. In the Holy Roman Empire, his first instinct was to condemn Luther unseen, and their meeting at the Diet of Worms concluded with a forthright declaration against Luther. In 1523 Charles's hereditary dominions, the Netherlands, saw the first executions for Protestant beliefs anywhere in Europe.

The 16th century would be the Habsburg century, and therein lay the Church's salvation. As Charles V passed the core of his massive dominions to his son Philip II, the tradition of Catholic loyalty would continue undiminished. But by then the Church had finally found its voice: the Counter-Reformation was in full swing.

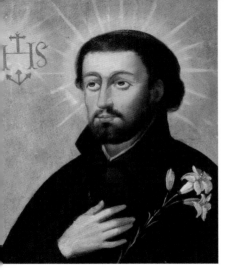

The Council of Trent

The deliberations of the Council of Trent decisively set the limits of acceptable theological belief in the 16th century. The Council had been a long time in preparation, and the council's deliberations took over 20 years, but its eventual achievement was considerable, providing the solid theological and institutional core for the long-desired movement of Catholic renewal.

Francis Xavier, Jesuit saint and apostle to Asia. The Jesuits embodied the commitment and fervour needed to combat the insidious spread of Protestantism in Europe and to carry forth the missionary effort to the newly discovered lands of Asia and the Americas.

This artistic representation of the concluding session of the Council of Trent in 1564 is found in a 17th-century painting. After an uncertain and sparsely attended opening, the glittering closing ceremony was a tangible symbol of the council's success. Three sessions spread over 20 years had rearmed Catholicism for the struggle against heresy.

Emperor Charles V favoured a meeting under his influence in Germany, but successive popes were determined on an Italian location. Trent (now Trento), within the borders of the Holy Roman Empire, but in the Italian-speaking enclave south of the Alps, eventually satisfied both parties.

When the council finally met the pomp of the opening procession on 13 December 1545 only barely disguised a disappointing turn-out. But the assembled Church fathers persevered, through long discussions and, at times, heated argument. By the time the council closed some 20 years later, they had achieved that comprehensive definition of Catholic belief that the Church so badly needed.

The first substantive decision of the Council of Trent was to affirm the validity of the Latin Vulgate: a peremptory repudiation of years of Protestant (and humanist) criticism of the venerable received text of the Bible. The following year, the Council adopted a decree on justification equally unequivocal in its forthright rejection of Luther's perception of justification by faith alone, and went on to affirm the canonicity of the seven sacraments (Protestants recognized only two). The fathers also affirmed the continuing

value of tradition alongside the authority of Scripture. The second period, 1551–2, produced a landmark declaration affirming transubstantiation. These doctrinal debates dominated the early sessions. It was only in the last sessions of 1561–3 that the bishops were able finally to conclude the decrees on Church reform that would shape the Church's approach to internal renewal over the following centuries: strengthening the authority of bishops over chapters and colleges, ordering episcopal visitations, and reform of religious orders and clerical discipline.

The Jesuits and new orders

In the history of the Counter-Reformation, a special place is always reserved for the new religious orders and, first and foremost, the Jesuits. The vision that lay behind the foundation of the Jesuits was that of a Basque nobleman, Ignatius Loyola. Loyola had dedicated his life to the Church after an early career as a soldier. When, in 1528, he settled in Paris to pursue his theological studies, he soon collected around him a small company of like-minded individuals, among them his fellow Basque, Francis Xavier. Together the group practised the rigorous programme of worship and self-examination devised by Ignatius, immortalized as his *Spiritual Exercises*.

Ordained priests in 1537, in 1540 Ignatius and his followers were formally constituted as the Society of Jesus, dedicated to an active life of preaching and ministry, and acknowledging absolute and direct obedience to the pope. The principles embodied by Loyola – meticulous preparation and training, unwavering obedience, and a religious life of active service outside the cloister – proved an inspiration and lifeline to an embattled Church. Loyola's fame ensured a steady stream of new adepts. By the time of his death in 1556, the original group of ten members had grown to 1500, and this number would increase tenfold by the end of the century. All novices who joined the order would be required to follow the full course of the *Spiritual Exercises*. The training was hard, and many did not last the course, but those who did emerged fully committed to the order's primary goals of preaching, teaching, and

Peter Paul Rubens, The Miracle of Ignatius Loyola. *This baroque representation was a far cry from the austerity preached by the first Jesuits and epitomized in the career and writings of their founder, Ignatius Loyola. The search for new saints, however, was an essential part of the repudiation of Protestant values and the ornate splendour of the Baroque its visual manifestation.*

conversion. Jesuits eschewed the parochial ministry for service in schools, hospitals, and the mission field, and also at court, for the order soon counted a number of Europe's crowned heads among their most fervent admirers.

The efforts of the Jesuits were seconded by other new orders that emerged from this era of turbulence and self-examination within Catholicism. The Capuchins began as an offshoot of the Italian Observant movement, and they spread rapidly through the peninsula during the 1530s. The order made its name in works of charity and in preaching. The Theatrines, founded in Rome in 1524, dedicated themselves to ministry and liturgical reform. The re-examination of the vocation of the female religious life also led to significant new initiatives, notably the foundation in 1532 of the Company of St Ursula (the Ursulines). It is significant that so many of these new initiatives emanated from Italy, and there can be little doubt that this active revivalism played an important role in deflecting the movement of evangelical reform within the peninsula from a more profound engagement with Protestantism.

It was in the field of education that the Jesuits left their most profound mark. There were seven Jesuit colleges in existence by 1544; by 1565, there were 30 colleges in Italy alone, and new foundations were carrying Jesuitism towards places like Prague and Poland. In the first generation, the most important role of the new religious orders was providing a model of inspirational service: of sacrifice, if necessary unto death. To Europe's Catholics, desperate for clear guidance in a world where the familiar was under threat, the new orders offered patient certainties and unflinching resistance to the Church's foes. Further afield, inspiration was provided by men like Francis Xavier, who in 1542 embarked on the first of his missions to the non-Christian world: India, from where he established Goa as a base for Jesuit operations in Asia, and latterly in Japan. Missionary successes provided some compensation for the losses suffered to Protestantism closer to home.

The Wars of Religion

The second half of the 16th century brought a new and murderous intensity to the religious conflicts that characterized the age. The rise of Calvinism and the emergence of Counter-Reformation Catholicism brought two strong, self-confident and mutually incompatible faiths into conflict. The result was to plunge Northern and Western Europe into 40 years of turmoil, culminating in the infamous massacres of Paris and Antwerp, before peace was finally restored.

France

The first country to feel the effects of new developments was Calvin's own homeland, France. Calvin had left France in 1536; however, as his ministry in Geneva became more firmly established, he never forgot the suffering evangelicals of his homeland. By 1555, the steady infiltration of Calvinist ideas was beginning to have its effect in France. Churches were established in many of France's largest cities. Despite continuing persecution by the Catholic authorities, these churches grew steadily in size and self-confidence, urged on by Calvin's encouragement and more tangible help in the form of ministers dispatched from Geneva to lead them.

Then, in a few months in 1558–9, the prospects of the movement changed dramatically. In England, the Catholic queen Mary died, to be replaced by the Protestant Elizabeth. This shift in the geopolitical balance was confirmed when Henry II of France was fatally wounded at a tournament to celebrate the peace with Spain. The succession of his 15-year-old son Francis II unleashed a power struggle at court

that bitterly exacerbated existing religious tensions. For the first time, leading nobles openly associated themselves with calls for religious toleration.

When Francis II in turn died unexpectedly (of an ear abscess, in December 1560), a new government, led by the Queen Mother, Catherine de Medici, attempted to pacify the new Calvinist Church, since 1555 grown to a mass movement of over 1000 congregations and one million members. It was not to be. The Colloquy of Poissy of 1561, a meeting of Catholic bishops and Calvinist pastors aimed at providing for a settlement, broke up without agreement. When Catherine went ahead and proclaimed limited toleration anyway, outraged Catholics took to arms. The massacre of a Protestant congregation at Vassy in March 1562 gave the signal for a general conflict.

The wars unleashed in 1562 would last for 36 years. During this time, the fighting was far from continuous. There would be seven bursts of military activity, none lasting more than two years. Once the fighting had commenced, however, it proved almost impossible to rebuild any sense of trust. The well-meaning peace settlements concluded after each conflict repeatedly collapsed under the pressure of events. For this was, from the beginning, an international conflict.

Scotland

After France, the first to feel the consequence of the new political constellation was Scotland, where the accession of a Protestant regime in England emboldened a small group of dissident Scottish nobles, urged on by John Knox, to establish Protestant worship. By the end of the year, evangelicals had seized churches in several Scottish burghs and forced the French regent Mary of Guise to take refuge in Edinburgh castle. When English troops intervened on the Protestant side, victory was assured, and the Scottish revolution had created an unlikely triumph for the Reformation.

The staunchly Catholic king Philip II of Spain was determined to suppress the spread of Calvinism in the Netherlands. His harsh measures, combined with heavy taxes, led to a general revolt. In 1579, ten Catholic provinces in the south were rallied to the Spanish cause by the promise of political liberty (the Union of Arras). A few days later, seven Calvinist provinces in the north formed the Union of Utrecht, splitting the country in two. In a truce in 1609 Spain conceded their independence.

The Dutch Revolt 1568-1609
- Extent of Spanish Netherlands 1568
- Union of Arras 1579
- Joined Union of Utrecht 1579 and 1581
- Limit of Spanish advance 1589
- Netherlands in terms of 1609 truce
- Boundary of Holy Roman Empire 1568

Revolt in the Netherlands

All of these events could only make difficulties for Philip II, whose northern territories in the Netherlands now looked dangerously exposed. In 1559 Philip abandoned his northern domains and returned to Spain. He left behind a land whose population was nursing an increasing sense of grievance at foreign, Spanish rule.

The Low Countries, too, were beginning to be unsettled by the spreading Calvinist heresy. Many of its inhabitants (particularly in the southern Walloon provinces where French was the predominant language) had friends and relatives in France, and reports of the violence and disruption there spread quickly across the frontier. Soon Calvinist cells were active in all of the major towns of Flanders and Brabant, encouraged by ministers who moved easily back and forth across the Channel to safe havens in Protestant England.

The dissidents' pleas for toleration were increasingly echoed by members of the nobility, led by William of Orange, who were happy to use the religious question as a stick with which to beat Philip's unfortunate regent, Margaret of Parma. When Philip, in Spain, firmly rejected her recommendation to exhibit more moderation in his pursuit of heresy, the nobility staged a mass demonstration of defiance, riding armed into Margaret's chamber in Brussels.

Margaret had little choice but to give way, and, in April 1566, she ordered a temporary suspension of the heresy laws. The Calvinists thought their hour had come. Hurrying back from their exile in towns abroad to join the growing congregations, in the summer of 1566 they staged a series of mass open-air sermons – the so-called "hedge-preaching". In August, they went a step further. Sensing the opportunity to force the issue, small bands were sent into the churches to strip them of their Catholic statues and images, and cleanse them for Protestant worship.

The controlled violence of the iconoclasm initially achieved its objective: cowed town councils hastened to make buildings available for the Protestant congregations. But it also destroyed the loose opposition coalition that had united the nobility and the Protestant ministers. Shocked by the radicalism of what had occurred, the nobles drew back and assisted Margaret of Parma in putting down the Calvinist insurrection by force. By 1567, the churches were shut up and the Calvinists forced back into exile.

If Philip now felt that the problem of rebellion in the Netherlands had been solved, his hopes were premature. He took a decisive and fatal step when he dispatched to the Netherlands his most distinguished general, the Duke of Alva, to replace the exhausted Margaret as regent. Alva interpreted his instructions to punish the guilty with a severity that created thousands of new converts to the cause.

The Calvinists, secure in their exile strongholds, were able to make effective war on Alva through a campaign of privateering that preyed on the vital seaborne trade of the Netherlands. Soon the Netherlands was plunged into an economic crisis rendered more severe by the taxes Alva demanded to pay for the occupying army.

When, in 1572, a small group of rebel troops descended on the coast of Holland, most towns in the northern province soon opened their gates. Alva was compelled to subjugate them by force, but a brutal campaign of sieges failed to dislodge them. The valiant resistance of Leiden, inspired by the leadership of William of Orange, finally broke the spirit of the Spanish troops. Unpaid and disgruntled, thousands mutinied in 1576 and descended on Antwerp in search of loot. The richest city of the Netherlands was plundered in three days of lawless violence that left thousands dead in the Sack of Antwerp. The outraged Dutch now banded together in an alliance – the Pacification of Ghent – dedicated to expelling the Spaniards once and for all.

The Catholic retaliation

In France, the first religious war had ended after a year of inconclusive fighting. The prospects for reconciliation looked relatively good. An optimistic

Philip II by Titian, an allegory of the Battle of Lepanto. To Philip of Spain fell the responsibility to defend the Catholic faith on several fronts: against Protestant heresy in the north and west, against the Ottomans in the Mediterranean. His victory over the Turks at Lepanto in 1571 was his finest hour, celebrated throughout Europe as a decisive blow in the defence of Christendom.

Portrait of Henry II, King of France, and his wife, Catherine de Medici. The death of Henry II in 1559 would plunge France into crisis. His widow, Catherine, would remain a figure of political influence through the reign of three sons and three decades of religious warfare.

engaged the loyalty of many Huguenots in France, and now their most distinguished commander, Admiral Coligny, urged Charles IX to intervene in the Netherlands on the Protestant side. Catholics recoiled in horror, and Catherine, alarmed at Coligny's influence over the young Charles IX, was persuaded to take action to avoid an entanglement that would have meant certain war against Spain. A bungled assassination attempt against Coligny led to the fatal order for a pre-emptive strike against the Huguenot leaders gathered in Paris for the royal wedding. The attack, enthusiastically supported by the fanatically Catholic population of Paris, turned into an indiscriminate slaughter that became one of the most notorious crimes of the century: the St Bartholomew's Day Massacre, in which thousands of Huguenots were killed in Paris.

The events in Paris devastated the Huguenot leadership and accelerated a process of decline for French Protestantism that had begun with the Huguenot failure to win the first religious war. But the Church survived, secure in strongholds in the south of France, far from royal power. However, for all the bold words of Huguenot resistance theory, the fate of the movement was essentially decided: French Protestantism would survive, but as a minority movement. The opportunity for the conversion of France was gone.

In the Netherlands, too, these years brought an improvement of Catholic prospects. Chastened by the calamities of 1576, Philip's representatives adopted a more conciliatory tone, and this soon began to erode the fragile unity of the revolt. In 1579, a group of the southern provinces was persuaded to renew their loyalty to Spain in the Union of Arras. When the northern rebel provinces responded with their own Union of Utrecht, the future division of the Netherlands into a free north – the United Provinces or Dutch Republic – and a Spanish south – in modern-day Belgium – emerged.

Only military action could resolve the situation, and in the Duke of Parma the Spaniards had the finest general of the age. When Philip of Spain at last committed the necessary resources, the Spanish armies won some significant victories. Successive campaigning seasons brought the capitulation of most of the major cities of the southern plains, culminating in 1585 with the fall of Antwerp.

The resolution of the Reformation conflict

The assassination of William of Orange in 1584 and the fall of Antwerp plunged the Dutch Revolt into crisis. To sustain the revolt, Elizabeth I of England finally pledged military aid: the long-delayed showdown with Philip of Spain drew ever closer. English troops in the Netherlands did

Catherine de' Medici concluded the Peace of Amboise in 1560, promising limited toleration for the Protestant Huguenots, and immediately embarked on a two-year tour of France to introduce the young Charles IX to his people.

But in too many parts of France, the Catholics and Huguenots now hated each other with a passion, and the smallest incident could set off violence once more. In the event, the spark for renewed fighting came from outside the kingdom. The passage of the Duke of Alva's army to the Netherlands raised fears among Protestants everywhere. In France, the jittery Huguenot nobles once more took to arms, in two further bursts of fighting, in 1567–8 and 1568–70, which were ended by a new peace with the Treaty of St Germain in 1570.

Once again, Catherine attempted to construct a coalition for peace, now to be sealed by the marriage of her daughter, King Charles IX's sister, Margaret de Valois to the titular head of the Huguenot movement, the young Henry of Navarre (later Henry IV). But events again conspired to thwart these good intentions. The struggle of the Dutch Calvinists had

The Massacre of the Innocents

Dutch painter Pieter Brueghel the Elder (c.1525–69) lived through the turbulent events of the Dutch Revolt, and this darkly moving picture is often thought to be a veiled commentary on that period. Brueghel takes the well-known Nativity tale of the massacre of the first-born ordered by Herod and reinterpets it as a winter landscape. But here the tranquil beauty of the town is destroyed by murderous and pillaging soldiers, watched by a black-armoured commander, sometimes taken to be the Duke of Alva. Events like this were a frequent feature of the Dutch Revolt, and hatred of the Spanish soldiers eventually led the provinces to unite and throw off Spanish rule.

enough to persuade Philip that the final defeat of the Netherlands would occur only if England were subdued first.

This was the genesis of the famous Armada campaign of 1588: in effect, an attempt to solve the whole complex of problems of Northern Europe. In France, Philip could be assured of the support of the resurgent Guise family, now united in their hostility to the succession of a Huguenot king, Henry of Navarre, heir since the death of the last Valois brother, the Duke of Anjou, in 1584. In the Netherlands, the Duke of Parma was ordered to suspend his campaign and to prepare to embark his battle-hardened troops for England.

The strategic ambition was impressive, but the consequence of failure calamitous. As the Armada limped home, scattered by English fire-ships and adverse weather, Philip's entire position began to unravel. In France, King Henry III, emboldened by Philip's humiliation, made one last effort to free himself from the powerful Guise family. In December 1588, he summoned the Duke of Guise and his brother the Cardinal and had them assassi-nated. When Henry was himself murdered by an avenging member of the Catholic League (an association of Catholic princes of the Holy Roman Empire), Henry of Navarre became Henry IV.

It would take Henry a further five years finally to quell the League and make good his claim to the throne. Philip made frantic efforts to prevent his victory, twice ordering the Duke of Parma to march his army south from the Netherlands to assist the League. But this merely afforded the hard-pressed Dutch breathing space, and, by 1594, the survival of an independent Dutch state was assured.

In France, Henry IV's victory came at a cost. A realist, he recognized that he could not govern without taking the religion of the majority of his subjects, and, in 1593, he converted to Catholicism. The settlement with his former Huguenot allies in 1598, the Edict of Nantes, allowing freedom of worship, brought the French civil wars to an end. The conflicts in France, the Netherlands, and Britain had brought war and hardship for more than a generation, but they had effectively settled the religious map of Western Europe for the next three centuries.

Titian, Portrait of Charles V. *This portrait was made in 1533, the year the Italian painter was called to the court of Charles V, where he was appointed court painter.*

THE HIGH RENAISSANCE

In the early Renaissance, Italy had no rival as the cultural centre of Europe. Europe's rulers vied for the service of Italy's best-known artists and architects, legendary figures such as the painters Sandro Botticelli in Florence and Giovanni Bellini in Venice, and the sculptor Donatello. Gradually, however, the influence of Italian culture spread through the continent; by the end of the 16th century, German, French, and Dutch artists could equal the best that Italy had to offer.

Italy

The last three decades of the 15th century were a wondrous time in the history of the arts. In these years, the culture of the Italian city-states reached its apogee: the proud cities of Florence, Venice, and Milan vied for supremacy, and the wealth of their leading citizens was poured out in an extravagant rebuilding and redecoration of the urban environment. These were great years for artists and architects. In Florence, the distinctive style of Sandro Botticelli gave way to that of Filippo and Filippino Lippi. Waiting in the wings was the prodigious genius of the young Raphael.

By the end of the century, the power of Florence declined, as successive French invasions exposed the vulnerability of the smaller independent states. But the eager cultural patronage of a succession of ambitious popes ensured a new source of lucrative commissions in Rome. Raphael and Michelangelo were both employed on the redecoration of the new Papal Palace and St Peter's Cathedral, with Michelangelo devoting the last 20 years of his life to his master work, the Sistine Chapel.

Northern Europe

The French invasions brought turmoil and destruction to many parts of the Italian peninsula. But the consequences in artistic terms were far from wholly detrimental. The presence of invading armies from northern Europe exposed many of these newcomers to the wonders of Italian art and civilization. A succession of French kings aspired equally both to establish territories on Italian soil, and to export the best of Italian artists to work in their own courts. For Leonardo da Vinci, the result was a comfortable, pampered French retirement; for French architecture the consequence was a new stylistic revolution that combined the best of northern Gothic style with the lessons of the Italian domestication of the Classics.

The close commercial connections between Italy and the rising cities of south Germany also played their part in spreading the artistic breakthroughs of Italian Renaissance north of the Alps. When Albrecht Dürer returned to Germany from his study trips in the studios of Florence and Venice the impact of his new woodcut series on the German public was sensational. In the years that followed Germany would come to take the lead in the development of the new woodcut art, as printmaking moved out from the artist's studio into a generalized book culture.

Cross-fertilization

But this was pre-eminently an age in which cultural cross-fertilization embraced all of the central populated landmass of Europe. Encouraged by the growth of a new European book market in the first century after the invention of printing, scholars and artists in all parts of Europe became accustomed to seeking their models and exemplars both from a local vernacular tradition and from the great schools of other European cultures.

What was true of painting, sculpture and architecture was even more obvious in the field of literature. Here the pre-eminently transnational tradition of Humanism combined with a general admiration of Italian letters to create new and intellectually interdependent school of literature, poetry, and drama.

The Northern Renaissance

The development of the northern Renaissance in no way submerged the admiration of things Italian. The French armies that descended on the peninsula left a trail of plunder, but their kings maintained a profound respect for Italian art and craftsmanship. Artistic visitors to Italy ensured that the new discoveries of the Renaissance – the mastery of perspective and the realistic rendering of the human form – did not remain confined to the peninsula.

The Renaissance in France

Louis XII and Francis I continued to look to Italy for cultural models, and many of Italy's leading artists were tempted north by their offer of salaries and lucrative commissions. Andrea del Sarto and Benvenuto Cellini were among those who worked for Francis I, and Leonardo da Vinci was able to trade his reputation for an affluent retirement in France.

For all the eager imitation of all things Italian, the most enduring legacy of this French Renaissance would be the distinctive style of architecture. France's kings lavished enormous energy on the rebuilding of their castles and residences, evolving in the process a unique style that merged classical Italian principles with those of the northern tradition. The châteaux of the Loire exuded the confidence of a

new monarchy that no longer required their places of residence to be fortified for defence. It was a style of architectural statement that was in turn widely imitated throughout Europe, and in French urban architecture. The models were freely available in lavishly illustrated architectural textbooks, one of the many new classes of luxury book.

Germany and the Netherlands

One of the first to carry the artistic techniques of the Rreniassance back to a northern context was the precocious German artist Albrecht Dürer. Dürer brought the lessons of Italian technique to bear on the naturalistic German tradition of painting with its deeply felt interest in landscape – known as the Danube school. Dürer was a genuine innovator. He excelled

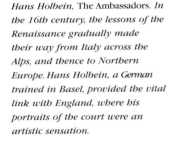

Hans Holbein, The Ambassadors. *In the 16th century, the lessons of the Renaissance gradually made their way from Italy across the Alps, and thence to Northern Europe. Hans Holbein, a German trained in Basel, provided the vital link with England, where his portraits of the court were an artistic sensation.*

not only in the conventional modes of panel painting, but also in the new forms of woodcut and metal engraving. His two great woodcut series, the so called *"Large" Passion* and the *Life of Maria*, were among the great artistic achievements of the age. Dürer also excelled in the commercial exploitation of his genius, not least in this new graphic art. Sets of the woodcuts changed hands for considerable sums; there was a world of difference between these and the cheap prints hawked on the streets or from booksellers' stalls in the marketplace.

The woodcut, an illustrative form capable of mass production, was German art's distinctive contribution to the Renaissance. It revolutionized the artistic production of a tradition already in a state of transition where the established worlds of mediaeval Gothic art faced the new discoveries of the Renaissance. The darkly brooding intensity of the late Gothic masters, epitomized by the work of Matthias Grünewald, gave way to a host of artist entrepreneurs, whose work was characterized by an enormous variety of modes and styles – among them Albrecht Altdorfer of Regensburg and Lucas Cranach at Wittenberg. Lucas Cranach would win enduring fame as the painter of the Reformation. An early and enthusiastic convert to the doctrines of his close friend Martin Luther, Cranach documented the transformation of the shy monk into the religious prophet and patriarch of Protestantism in a series of wonderfully evocative portrait studies. These were replicated in mass production in Cranach's busy Wittenberg workshop to hang in the new Protestant burgher households of Germany: one of the first fully documented instances of the use of art to produce a propagandistic image. The shrewd Cranach also played his part in the development of the book art of the new Protestant movement. His contribution to woodcut design is best known for the series of images that embellished Luther's new German Bible, but of equal significance was his role in the development of the decorated title-page: fine ornate borders that to their potential readers identified the book with its evangelical contents as clearly as a modern trademark or logo.

None grasped the new potential of the marketplace better than Hans Holbein the Younger. Holbein settled first in Basle, then, when the Reformation threatened the market in Church art, in England. He became court painter to Henry VIII, producing a series of portraits of nobles and courtiers in a modern style previously unknown in England. Typically for a Renaissance court artist, Holbein's work for Henry included eclectic commissions such as the decoration of furniture, designs for precious vases, and book illustration. The concept of the artist as master of an individual style – rather than the talented artisan working to order – emerged only gradually.

Lucas Cranach the Elder's 1534 "Creation of the World" woodcut, an endpaper from the Luther Bible. Cranach worked closely with with Martin Luther on his bible and pamplets, but this did not preclude him from also working for Catholic patrons.

In the Netherlands the rich artistic tradition inherited from Burgundian Flanders suffered a rude interruption with the Protestant assault on art during the Dutch Revolt. In Holland the fury of the iconoclasts was so intense that little survives: this is almost a lost age of Dutch art. The meticulously observed paintings of Brueghel did something to revive the tradition, and look ahead to a new age of genre painting that would come to full fruition only with the commercial art market of the 17th century Dutch Republic.

This relative hiatus in the visual arts was balanced by a distinctive Netherlandish cultural contribution with the dramatic productions of the *Rederijckerkamers*, or Chambers of Rhetoric. The Chambers were dramatic societies, often based on an occupational group, who met together to explore moralistic or theological themes through dramatic performance. In this respect they were ideal vehicles for the expression of covert dissent, and the Chambers often ran into trouble with the church authorities. Despite this they survived into the 17th century, where they faced a new challenge from Calvinist criticism of the theatre. The same was true of England, where the birth of a commercial theatre in London heralded a great age in the history of dramatic composition. The era of the Swan, the Globe and other London open-air theatres was remarkably brief, little more than 60 years (1580–1640), but the genius of Shakespeare and Marlowe established the reputation of English letters for all time.

The Renaissance in Italy

It says much for the resilience of Italian society that it was able to emerge from the serial calamities of the French wars and the devastation of the Sack of Rome in 1527, and remain a beacon for all educated Europeans committed to the arts and humane letters. Though war had taken its toll on great patrons such as the Medici, the infrastructure of cultural life remained robust.

Michelangelo's David. *Created to epitomize the values of a proud city-state, Michelangelo's exuberant celebration of the human form formed a massive and tangible expression of the values of both the humanist movement and the Renaissance.*

Titian became the ultimate high-society portraitist, travelling widely from one European court to another. This 1539 portrait of Francis I of France, however, was painted without his having ever seen his model in real life, using a medal made by Benvenuto Cellini instead.

The French wars had left Italian society battered and its cities scarred by decades of turmoil and the incursion of invading armies. The destruction reached its climax with the Sack of Rome in 1527. While the armies of the Holy Roman Emperor, Charles V, looted the city, the Pope was an effective prisoner of the Emeror in the Castel Sant' Angelo. The humiliation of Italy was complete.

Despite this onslaught, however, Italian universities managed to preserve their reputation as leaders in the technical subjects of law and medicine, and students continued to flock to Padua, Bologna and Ferrara from all over Europe, even from nations that had embraced Protestantism. In this respect it was a great blessing for Italian culture that the peninsula was spared the most bitter religious divisions that afflicted northern Europe in the second half of the century. Safely, if somewhat cynically anchored within the Roman church, its scholars could pursue a humanist agenda with little of the polemic that blighted scholarship in northern Europe.

This was a great age of both literary composition, and print culture, both drawing their inspiration from the enduring appeal of the Classics. While Italian publishers cemented their reputation as Europe's leading producers of editions of Roman and Greek scholarship, dramatists and poets created a notable new generation of literary works, many of them eagerly taken up in other European lands, where Italian literary culture was still both admired and imitated.

The most enduring monuments to the culture of Italy would remain the traditional fields of architecture and the arts. In the wake of the sack of Rome a succession of Popes set abut remodelling the city, an architectural reconsecration of the centre of Christendom. Naples, too, was remodelled as a capital of the Spanish south; in Florence and Venice leading citizens continued to display their eminence in buildings of opulence and style. But even here there was a change of emphasis, as the function of an ornate façade evolved from advertising the building behind to organizing the public space in front: described by one scholar as a shift from architecture to urban planning.

The Visual Arts

The artistic tradition of the 16th century required no radical departures. Fidelity to the style of the great masters of the earlier era, such as Raphael, ensured one measure of continuity; the longevity of men such as Michaelangelo (who lived until 1568) was another. It was also the case that some of the largest artistic or architectural projects stretched over so long a period that the imprint of the earlier era was necessarily more enduring. Successive architects of the Palazzo Farnese in Rome all remained faithful to the original plans of 1514.

Nevertheless changing times did leave their imprint on artistic style. The challenge of Protestantism reinforced the importance of the papacy as the focus of the Catholic Church. The growing confidence of Catholic renewal after the

Paolo Veronese's "Feast in the House of Levi", 1573, was intended as a vision of the Last Supper. The painter was forced to rename the work to appease the religious authorities, who regarded his inclusion of dogs, a cat, midgets, Huns, and drunken revelers as blasphemous.

Council of Trent brought the development of new, self-consciously opulent forms of devotional art. In Italy, this was the age of the High Renaissance and Mannerism, epitomized by the dominance of the Venetian school. Its best-known figure, Titian, was an artist of truly international reputation. A talented student of Giovanni Bellini, he made his reputation partly by completing a number of unfinished commissions after the death of his master; he became in the process, an acknowledged genius of the art of fresco painting. Over the following decades Titian expanded this reputation to embrace religious and mythological paintings and portraiture. One of his most enduring monuments is a series of great altarpieces for Italian patrons, though Titian was by now known, and in great demand, all over Europe. He travelled widely, fulfilling commissions for both Charles V and Philip II, as well as successive popes. His free and expressive brushwork had a profound influence on later artists, particularly his successors in the Venetian school, Tintoretto and Paulo Veronese.

In contrast to the well travelled Titian, the best of Tintoretto's work was created for local Venetian patrons, and most of his work can only be seen in the churches and civic buildings for which they were painted. These commissions include the remarkable series of decorative paintings for the Scuola di San Rocco that occupied him for almost 20 years from 1565: scenes from the life of Christ in the upper hall, and the life of the Virgin in the lower. The scale and boldness of this conception epitomized the genius of Tintoretto. He was an extraordinary draughtsman, and by his own account he attempted to combine "the drawing of Michaelangelo with the colour of Titian". He also followed Titian in the quality of the portraits he produced.

While Tintoretto worked in the Scuola Paolo, Veronese was occupied on a similarly grandiose scheme in the ducal palace. Veronese was one of the greatest of all decorative artists, combining a sense of pageant with a keen eye for the evocative human detail. His deep interest in the architectural structure of painting was reflected in the monumental marble columns that frame, often incongruously, mythological and biblical scenes. This evoked a measure of criticism, even in Veronese's own day. Although he stubbornly defended the artistic licence he regarded as the proper attribute of the creative imagination, his penchant for crowded feast scenes drew him into controversy after the design for a Last Supper in the Academia brought him a summons from the Venetian Inquisition. Rather than evoking the solemn dignity of this seminal scene, the religious authorities charged that his insistence on crowding the painting with irrelevant and frivolous figures amounted to a calculated act of blasphemy. Veronese resolved the issue by renaming the picture *Feast in the House of Levi*.

Veronese's brush with religious orthodoxy was an early indication of the problems that would later dog the free-wheeling genius Caravaggio. More representative of the new religiosity was El Greco, born in Crete but active for the first part of his career mostly in Rome. In 1577 two commissions brought him to Toledo, and to the attention of his most influential patron, Philip II of Spain. The tormented spirituality of his figures were an effective metaphor for the fervent introspective faith of this most devoted son of the church, and El Greco's future was secure, both as a painter of religious subjects and as an unusual, and highly expressive portrait artist.

The decoration of Philip II's new palaces opened a new age of patronage in Spain, a role echoed at other great courts of central Europe. With the growth of new capitals in Vienna and Prague, the Habsburgs would therefore end the century as they had begun: as the most significant artistic patrons of the age.

Technological and Intellectual Progress

The 16th century was not a period of startling technological change: none of the transforming scientific inventions or discoveries can be dated to this period. It did witness a steady advance in the sophistication of scientific enquiry, however, as men of learning turned enquiring minds towards the natural world, the human body, and the heavens.

Scientific enquiry in the 16th century could broadly be said to fall within three traditions: the organic, or science of observation, which was based on analogies drawn from the natural world; the magical, which cast God in the role of the interpreter of nature; and the mechanistic, based on the notion of the universe as machine, working within a framework of regularity, permanence, and predictability. Although each tradition of scientific enquiry made its contribution to the advancement of knowledge, these approaches were not equally conducive to the growth of modern science.

Architecture and engineering

In the 16th, as in so many other periods of history, one of the greatest stimuli to scientific and technological ingenuity was warfare. Large sums of money were spent on equipping ever larger armies with more deadly weaponry, and in building fortifications to resist more powerful artillery. Military engineering was one of the great scientific disciplines of the age, pursued without regard to expense. Throughout Europe cityscapes were remodelled as communities sought to surround themselves with the new bastion fortifications necessary to protect the brittle medieval

Nicolaus Copernicus' 1543 map of the universe, showing his theory of the earth, the planets, and the zodiac circling the sun. Martin Luther was among those who rejected Copernicus' ideas, stating: "I believe in the Holy Scripture, since Joshua ordered the Sun, not the Earth, to stand still."

walls from battering by cannon fire. One consequence of these developments was that battles came to count for far less, if fortified strong-points remained intact: a siege, or series of sieges, offered the only hope of decisive victory. The need to move large armies and artillery trains also demanded major improvements in road networks, another task for Europe's growing band of specialist engineers. The skills of architects and builders were, in this respect, more sought after than any of Europe's other professions, and spawned a large and expensive technical literature.

Sixteenth-century medicine

In medicine, too, the art of war provided an unexpected focus for innovations in surgery and post-traumatic care. A new genre of surgical textbooks emerged, all dedicated to advice on helping men (and horses) survive the horrendous wounds inflicted by battlefield firearms. Many were lavishly illustrated by carefully executed woodcuts of the barbarous surgical appliances recommended for amputations and the extraction of gunshot. The emergence of this popular genre of printed books in fact hints at a subtle, and ultimately fruitful, shift in the balance of medical practice, from theory to palliative treatment based on observation.

The focus on anatomy, while pointing the way towards the future, did not bring instant breakthroughs in treatment. One of the most influential 16th-century authors was Andreas Vesalius (1514–64), professor of surgery and anatomy at Padua. Vesalius's famous anatomical treatise *De Humanis Corporis fabrica* of 1543 was based on studies of cadavers, but the observation – and glorification – of the human form remained within the framework of an essentially moralistic world view. The science of anatomy led to few significant breakthroughs in the treatment of illness and disease.

The wonderfully gifted German physician Paracelsus remained a maverick and an outsider. Paracelsus's criticism of the accepted orthodoxy of the 2nd-century Greek anatomist Galen to some extent anticipated a more modern school of organic treatment, moving beyond the Greek tradition that the roots of disease were to be found in a disordered balance of the four humours: phlegm, choler, melancholy, and blood. But his insistence on chemical remedies and faith in the Jewish cabbala plotted no clear route forward. Medical science advanced dramatically only with William Harvey's discovery of the circulation of the blood in the following century.

The Natural World

Significant progress was made in the 16th century in the science of observation, notably in the fields of

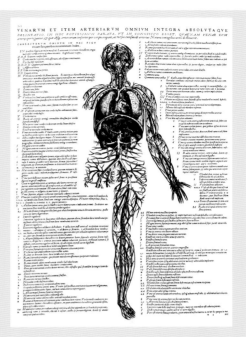

Sixteenth-century medicine

The system of the veins, a woodcut from Andreas Vesalis' *De Humani Corporis fabrica* (1543). Sixteenth-century medicine continued to be dominated by the conflicting theoretical systems of the ancients and remained too remote and academic to make much real improvement in the field of healthcare. But the ground was prepared for future breakthroughs by an increased interest in the observation of nature, here epitomized by the science of anatomy. Scholarly enquiry of this sort was indebted to the development of the woodcut, which provided the opportunity for the precise rendering of scientific observation.

anatomy and botany. The opening up of new continents further stimulated an already acute interest in the workings of the human body and the animal world. Especially influential was the work of the great German botanist Leonard Fuchs. In France, Pierre Belon published an influential series of studies, cast as travel narratives, based on close observation of the plant and animal kingdoms of Europe and Asia. Belon, like Fuchs, was deeply indebted to the illustrative woodcut, which reached its full potential in these works of scientific description. The woodcut, in fact, made a powerful and often underestimated contribution to the development of the scientific book.

Other classes of scientific book represented the constant search for ever more effective means of harnessing the world's natural resources. This reflected an enduring theme of the age: that technological change occurred not as a result of transforming invention, but through the incremental application of ever greater human ingenuity to existing technology. This was true in both the critical fields of mining and in the harnessing of wind and water power through mills and sail. Mining had long engaged some of Europe's most ingenious minds, though the great fortunes to be made encouraged a disregard for risk that made deep-shaft mining both perilous and backbreaking work. This found its most barbaric expression in the plundering of the huge reserves of silver discovered by Spanish explorers in the New World. Here, the exploitation of the indigenous peoples as labourers reached genocidal proportions.

An illustration of the dangerous activity of deep shaft mining from George Agricola's, De re metallica, *1556. Agricola was a doctor in the silver mining region around Freiburg, Germany. In his book he reviewed everything then known about mining, including equipment and machinery and means of finding ores. His book remained the standard work for another two centuries.*

The 16th century was an age of paradox, and nowhere was this more obvious than in the relationship between man and the natural world. Travel was still limited by the vagaries of wind and water, and by the capacities and endurance of men and horses, yet the period definitely witnesses a definable shift in the apprehension of the terrestrial world. This was partly due to the dogged explorations of the merchant adventurers and the *conquistadores*, but for those who remained in Europe a new sense of the world's potential became tangible through developments in cartography. Here, print, science, and exploration combined to produce striking advances. The hunger for knowledge was evident even before the great voyages, as early printers turned out multiple editions of Ptolemy's *Geographia*, a text almost 1500 years old. Within a hundred years the wisdom of the ancients had been banished for ever, and the more authentic shape of the great continental landmasses was clearly recognizable in the *Theatrum orbis terrarum* (1570) produced by the Flemish geographer Abraham Ortelius, the first recognizably modern world atlas. This was followed in short order by Gerard Mercator's *Atlas* (1595), and a host of national and regional projects. The developments in cartography marked a decisive step in the internal rationalization of space and distance, but also the emergence of a concept of borders as a defined place, rather than as a region or geographical feature: a significant mental shift that helped shape military conflict in the centuries to come.

Science and religion

Other scientific investigators concentrated on three main fields: mathematics, astrology, and alchemy. All had strongly theological agendas. The science of numbers also had strong links with the cabbala, a connection embodied in the career of the Elizabethan scientist-magician John Dee. Dee epitomized the strangely ambiguous world of 16th-century science, combining a profound fascination with the wisdom of the ancients and an acute interest in observation and experiments. Thus the critical experiment of Galileo – his analysis of the acceleration of falling bodies – was partly anticipated by 16th-century figures, such as the Dutch mathematician and engineer Simon Stevin.

Much of the most profound and intense interest was devoted to the observation of the heavens and celestial bodies. The 16th century saw the first radical criticism of the geocentric theory of the universe inherited from Aristotle and Ptolemy. The Polish astronomer Nicolaus Copernicus revolutionized the traditional Ptolemaic cosmology by placing the sun at the centre of the universe, with the earth moving round it in an annual revolution. He also argued that the earth rotated on its axis every 24 hours.

These were extraordinary discoveries, but in his own day Copernicus was spurned, not least by the Protestant reformers Luther and Melanchthon, who preferred a science firmly grounded in the Bible. This is one of the many reasons why the scientific discoveries of the 16th century remained more potential than actual. This was an age caught between conflicting and mutually contradictory impulses. The wisdom of the ancients was simultaneously revered – by the humanists of the Renaissance – and distrusted. Many did not believe that God would have revealed the secrets of the universe to heathens. Much scientific energy was poured into alchemy, the search to transform base metal into gold. This deluded search at least built on the genuine, incremental technical advances in the manufacture of kilns and foundries, two of the real technological successes of the age. Most of all, however, the 16th century had as yet no place for a godless science – a science of observation made only halting progress against a world view based on spiritual and theoretical principles.

Political thought

More concrete were achievements in political thought. The political developments of a turbulent age stimulated men already attuned to fundamental questions of social organization by the acute observations of the ancients. Now talented thinkers applied these lessons to important contemporary developments, especially the rise of the state and the evolution of rival religious systems. The result was some notable theoretical writing, ranging from the broadly monarchist views of Claude de Seyssel and Jean Bodin, to the radical speculations of those who argued for a right of resistance to state power in defence of true religion. Fired by the bloody conflicts of the 16th century wars of religion, a number of influential figures in the Protestant churches, including Theodore de Bèze and the jurist François Hotman, dared to speculate under what circumstances it might be justifiable to overthrow a tyrant. These Protestant arguments found an unexpected echo in Catholic thought towards the end of the century, when the preachers of Paris sought to justify the rebellion of the Catholic League against Henry III. Such speculations were, however, against the grain in a society that found validating principles overwhelmingly in established custom. Most drew back from the radicalism and potential anarchy of empowering subjects to disobedience. .

"Africae Tabula Nova". An engraved map of the continent of Africa from Abraham Ortelius's, Theatrum Orbus Terrarum, *1570, the first atlas containing a uniform series of maps of the world.*

Biographies of Key Figures

Aquinas, St Thomas (1225–74): Italian philosopher, theologian, and Dominican friar; known as the "Angelic Doctor". Regarded as the greatest figure of scholasticism. Despite knowing no Greek or Hebrew, and hardly any history, through his commentaries he made Aristotle's thought available and acceptable in the Christian West. His *Summa Theologiae* (1266–73) is the greatest achievement of systematic medieval theology and includes his "five proofs" of the existence of God. His thought, with few exceptions, now represents the general teaching of the Catholic Church. Canonized in 1523. Feast day, 28 January.

Bernard of Clairvaux, St (1090–1153): French theologian and reformer. In 1113, entered the Cistercian order. His studious, ascetic life and stirring eloquence made him the oracle of Christendom. Founded more than 70 monasteries. The monks of his reformed branch of the Cistercians are often called Bernardines.

Boccaccio, Giovanni (1313–75): Italian writer, poet, and humanist. Famous for the *Decameron* (1348–58), a collection of 100 tales told by ten young people who have moved to the country to escape the Black Death. Influenced Chaucer, and was a lifelong friend of Petrarch.

Botticelli, Sandro born Alessandro di Mariano Filipepi (1445–1510): Florentine painter. Worked in Renaissance Florence under the patronage of the Medicis. Best known for his mythological works such as *Primavera* (*c*.1478) and *The Birth of Venus* (*c*.1480), both of which are in the Uffizi, Florence.

Brueghel, or **Breughel, Pieter the Elder** (*c*.1520–69): Flemish artist. Produced landscapes, religious allegories, and satires of peasant life. His work was highly regarded by Rubens, and his truthful rendering of peasant life and weather conditions sets his work apart from the more Italianate style of his Dutch contemporaries. Principal works include *The Blind Leading the Blind* (1568) and *The Peasant Wedding* (1568).

Calvin, John (1509–64): French Protestant theologian and reformer. On becoming a Protestant he fled to Switzerland, where he attempted to reorder society and established the first Presbyterian government in Geneva. His *Christianae Religionis Institutiae* (*Institutes of the Christian Religion*) of 1536 was the first systematized account of reformed Christian doctrine and ecclesiastical discipline.

Cervantes Saavedra, Miguel de (1547–1616): Spanish novelist and dramatist. Injured at the Battle of Lepanto, he turned to literature. His *Don Quixote*, published in two parts (1605, 1615), describes the adventures of a poor gentleman with inflated ideas of chivalry. A satire of human folly, it also possesses immense power of human sympathy, and has given the world some of its most famous stories. Immensely influential on European literature.

Charlemagne (742–814): Major post-Roman ruler of the West; conquered the Saxons, 772–804, and established his authority over northern Spain and northern Italy. Made his capital at Aix-la-Chapelle and crowned emperor of the West by Pope Leo III in Rome, 800. Regulated Church affairs and effected a general revival of prosperity and peace in the West.

Charles V (1500–58): King of Spain (as Charles I), 1516–56, Holy Roman Emperor, 1519–56. Vast inheritance of lands proved vulnerable to the rivalry of other powers and religious dissent aroused by Reformation. Career dominated by war, defending Christian Europe from the Turkish threat on land and at sea, struggling against Protestantism in Germany, rebellion in Castile, and war with France (1521–44). Defeated French at Pavia (1525), and Protestant forces at Mühlberg (1547). Exhausted by these struggles, Charles handed Naples, the Netherlands, and Spain over to his son Philip II, and the imperial crown to his brother Ferdinand, then retired to a monastery.

Cid, El, properly Rodrigo Diaz de Vivar (*c*.1043–99): Spanish warrior hero, immortalized as "El Cid" (The Lord). A vassal of Alfonso VI of Castile, he fought constantly from 1065. In 1081 he was banished for an unauthorized raid and began a long career as a soldier of fortune, serving both Spaniards and Moors. Beseiged and captured Valencia (1093–4) and became its ruler.

Columbus, Christopher (1451–1506): Genoese explorer and discoverer of the New World. Went to sea at 14 and fought in the Tunisian galleys. About 1470, shipwrecked off Cape St Vincent, reached Portugal on a plank. Conceived the idea of reaching India by sailing westward (and thus proving the world was round) as early as 1474, but plans not finally accepted, by Ferdinand and Isabella of Castile, until 1492. On 3 August, set sail in the *Santa Maria*, with the *Pinta* and *Niña*, and 120 men. Discovered various Caribbean islands, returning to Spain with full honours on 15 March 1493. Made several other voyages, discovering Dominica in the West Indies, and the South American mainland.

Copernicus, Nicolaus (1473–1543): Polish astronomer, and founder of modern astronomy. From 1491 studied mathematics, optics, and perspective at Kracow University, and in 1496, canon law at Bologna. In 1503, began the study of medicine at Padua, and was made doctor of canon law at Ferrara. In 1505, left Italy for Prussia, living at Frauenberg. His *De Revolutionibus Orbius Coelestium*, proving the sun to be the centre of the universe, was completed in 1530, and published just before his death in 1543.

Cortés, Hernán (1485–1547): Spanish conquistador and conqueror of Mexico. Landed on the coast of Mexico early in 1519. Exploited divisions between the Aztecs and their subjects, marching on Tenochtitlán, the site of present day Mexico City. Entered the city, abducted the Aztec king Montezuma, who was forced to submit as a vassal of Spain. In subsequent battles, he defeated Aztec armies, notably at Otumba in 1520, killing Montezuma. He was eventually deposed by his followers, but had established Spanish dominion in Mexico.

Dante Alighieri (1265–1321): Italian poet, born in Florence, a lawyer's son of the noble Guelf family. His lifelong love was Beatrice Portinari (*c*.1265–90); no evidence that she returned his love, and she married at an early age. As one of six priors of Florence, he showed characteristic sternness and impartiality to all the city's faction leaders. Sent on an embassy to Rome to Pope Boniface VIII in 1301, he never again set foot in his native town. Banished from Florence in 1309, and sentenced to death in absentia. Thenceforth led a wandering life, eventually settling in Ravenna, where he is buried. Married to Gemma Donati, Dante had six children. His most celebrated work is the *Divina Commedia*, begun around 1307, his spiritual testament, narrating a journey through hell and purgatory, guided by Virgil, and finally to paradise, guided by Beatrice.

Dürer, Albrecht (1471–1528): German painter and engraver. The leading German artist of the Renaissance, particularly important for his technically advanced woodcuts and copper engravings. Present at coronation of Charles V, who appointed him court painter. Met Luther during his later years, and showed great sympathy with the Reformation.

Elizabeth I (1533–1603): Queen of England, 1558–1603. Well-educated, survived early intrigues and imprisonment to emerge as one of Britain's most famous monarchs, principally for her defence of the country against Spanish invasion in the Armada of 1588 (and other later Armadas). Achieved a moderate religious settlement which survived her. Her reign was a delicate balance of negotiation and equivocation, England's European role limited by lack of finance. She never married.

Erasmus, Desiderius (*c*.1469–1536): Dutch humanist and scholar. The foremost Renaissance scholar of northern Europe; reacted against scholasticism and was drawn to the humanists. Although ordained a priest, paved the way for the Reformation with his satires on the Church, including the *Colloquia Familiaria* (1518). However he opposed the violence of the Reformation, and condemned Luther in *De Libero Arbitrio* (1525). Also published many popular, sometimes didactic works like the famous *Encomium Moriae* (*In Praise of Folly*, 1509). He taught in most of the cultural centres of Europe including Paris, Cambridge, and Oxford, meeting all the leading intellectuals of his day.

Ferdinand II (1452–1516): the first monarch of all Spain, as Ferdinand V of Castile, Ferdinand II of Aragon and Sicily, and Ferdinand III of Naples; known as "the Catholic". Marriage to Isabella of Castile united the Christian kingdoms of Spain. Established the Inquisition, 1478–80. Campaigned vigorously against the Moors, finally conquering Granada in 1492. In that same year, he expelled the Jews from the kingdom, and financed Christopher Columbus's expedition to the Americas, thus founding Spain's empire in the New World.

Francis of Assisi, St originally Giovanni Bernadone (1181–1226): Founder of the Franciscan order. Son of a wealthy Italian cloth merchant. In 1208 he rejected the world, adopting the complete observance of Christ-like poverty. His preaching friars travelled throughout Europe, founding new churches and monasteries.

Francis Xavier, St (1506–52): Spanish missionary, "the Apostle of the Indies". Studied, then lectured in Paris, becoming acquainted with Ignatius of Loyola, with whom he founded the Society of Jesus (1534). Ordained priest in 1537. Sent by John III of Portugal as missionary to the Portuguese colonies of the east; arrived at Goa in 1542. In 1548, founded a missionary in Japan that flourished for 100 years. Canonized in 1622.

Francis I (1494–1547): King of France from 151, and notable patron of the Renaissance. Met Henry VIII of England at the Field of the Cloth of Gold in 1520, a costly and portentous exercise that underlined the power and prosperity of France. His wars against HRE Charles V met with failure when he was captured at the Battle of Pavia in 1525, and only released the following year after renouncing his territorial claims.

Frederick I, Barbarossa (Redbeard) (*c*.1123–90): King of Germany and Holy Roman Emperor, 1152–90. Made sustained effort to subdue Italy and the papcy, but was eventually defeated at the Battle of Legnano in 1176. This led him to a policy of clemency and concession with his subjects. At the height of his power, led the Third Crusade against Saladin in 1189.

Galilei, Galileo, known as **Galileo** (1564–1642): Italian astronomer, mathematician, and natural philosopher, born in Pisa. Discovered the constancy of a pendulum's swing, formulated the laws of uniform acceleration of falling bodies, and described the parabolic trajectory of projectiles. Applying the telescope to astronomy, observed craters on the Moon, sunspots, four of Jupiter's satellites, and the phases of Venus. In 1632, published *Dialogo sopra i due massimi sistemi del mondo*, in favour of the Copernican system. After a long trial and imprisonment, sentenced to indefinite imprisonment by the Inquisition; sentence commuted by Pope Urban VIII. Thereafter he lived under house arrest at Arcetri near Florence, continuing researches despite severely impaired hearing and sight.

Giotto (Di Bodone) (*c*.1266–1337): Italian painter and architect. Artist in whose work the seeds of the Renaissance are to be found. Broke with the rigid conventions of Byzantine art and introduced a naturalistic style showing human expression. Among most important works are the frescoes in the Arena Chapel, Padua (1305–8), and the Peruzzi Chapel in the church of Santa Croce, Florence (*c*.1320). Appointed master of works for the cathedral and city of Florence in 1334.

Gregory VII, Hildebrand, St (*c*.1020–85): Became pope in 1073. The great representative of the temporal claims of the medieval papacy. Set about amending the secularized condition of the Church, particularly directing efforts against the practice of investiture. In response, the emperor Henry IV declared Gregory deposed, for which the pope excommunicated Henry. Henry set up a Clement III as antipope in 1080 (the Great Schism), and entered Rome in 1084 after a siege of three years. Gregory was rescued, but the wretched condition of Rome forced him to withdraw. He died in Salerno.

Gregory IX (1148–1241): Became pope in 1227. Constantly feuded with the emperor Frederick II, and asserted the highest view of papal power.

Henry IV (1553–1610): King of France and Navarre from 1589, first Bourbon monarch. Emerged as foremost Protestant commander in the French Wars of Religion. Succeeded to French throne after assassination of Henry III. Faced with the opposition of the Spanish-backed Catholic League, won important victories at Argues (1589) and Mayenne (1590). Forsook Protestantism to secure his position, but established security for Protestants in the Edict of Nantes. Secured peace with Spain at Vervins (1598), and set about rebuilding his country with his great minister Sully. Assassinated by a religious fanatic.

Holbein, Hans "the younger" (1497–1543): German painter and engraver. Painted great series of portraits of eminent Englishmen of his time, including Thomas More. Appointed court painter to Henry VIII in 1536, and painted portraits of the king's prospective wives. Most famous work is probably the portrait group *The Ambassadors*, in the National Gallery, London. Died of plague in London.

Ignatius Loyola, St (1491–1556): Spanish soldier, theologian and founder of the Society of Jesus. Having renounced military life, Loyola pursued the religious life with great zeal, founding the Society of Jesus with St Francis Xavier and four other associates in 1534. Originally aimed at encouraging pilgrimage to the Holy Land and conversion of the infidel, the rule of the order was approved by Pope Paul III in 1540, and Loyola's Spiritual Exercises (1534) is still used in the training of Jesuits today.

Ivan IV (1530–84): Grand duke of Muscovy, 1533–47, first tsar of Russia, 1547–84, known as "the Terrible". Established his personal authority and destroyed privileges of the boyar nobles. Captured Kazan, Astrakhan, and Siberia, but the Tartar siege of Moscow and Polish victory in the Livonian War (1558–82) left Russia weak and divided. Increasingly unstable, he flew into fierce rages, killing his son in 1581. Succession passed to his mentally handicapped second son Fyodor.

Leonardo da Vinci (1452–1519): Italian painter, architect, scientist, and engineer. Settled in Milan in 1482 where he painted his famous *Last Supper* in the refectory of the convent of Santa Maria delle Grazie. Entered the service of Cesare Borgia in Florence in 1500 as architect and engineer. Around 1504, he completed the *Mona Lisa*. 1506, employed by Louis XII of France; 1516, Francis I of France assigned him an annual allowance and the use of Château Cloux where he lived until his death. The outstanding all-round genius of the Renaissance, Leonardo had a knowledge and understanding far beyond his time in many fields including biology, anatomy, mechanics, and aeronautics, all demonstrated in his many notebooks.

Luther, Martin (1483–1546): German Protestant theologian, the principal figure of the German Reformation. Preached the doctrine of justification by faith rather than by good works, and attacked the sale of indulgences in his famous 95 theses (1517), and papal authority. Excommunicated at Diet of Worms in 1521. His translation of the Bible into High German (1522–34) contributed significantly to the development of German literature in the vernacular.

Magellan, Ferdinand (*c*.1480–1521): Portuguese navigator, leader of the first expedition to circumnavigate the globe. Served in the East Indies and was lamed for life in Morocco. Offering his services to Spain, he sailed from Seville on 10 August 1519 with five ships and 270 men. Having coasted Patagonia, he threaded the strait which bears his name and reached the ocean that he named the Pacific. By now one ship was wrecked, one had turned for home, a third was scuttled, and a fourth was captured by the Portuguese. Magellan himself was killed by natives in the Philippine islands. His ship, *Victoria*, was taken safely back to Spain by the last surviving Spanish captain, on 6 September 1522, to complete the circumnavigation of the world.

Michelangelo, properly **Michelagniolo di Lodovico Buonarroti** (1475–1564): Italian sculptor, painter, and poet. The most brilliant representative of the Italian Renaissance. Obsessively interested in the representation of the human body, whether in sculpture or painting. The Sistine Chapel in St Peter's, Rome, and his statue of *David*, in the Academy in Florence, represent these aims, influenced by classical examples, but their form and vitality render them far more than a simple neo-classicist imitation of the past.

Otto I (912–73): Emperor of Germany. Married to sister of Athelstan, King of England, 930; defeated the invasion of the French, 938, subjugating the Slavonians and Bohemians, 950. Invaded and subdued Italy and expelled the Hungarians from Germany. Crowned Emperor of the West, 962, he deposed the existing pope and nominated his own candidate, Leo VIII. Campaigned in southern Italy and defeated Harold II of Denmark the year before his death.

Philip II (1527–98): King of Spain from 1556, only son of HRE Charles V. One of the most powerful rulers of his day, he dedicated himself to the war against heresy (Protestantism), which involved him in ultimately unsuccessful wars in the Netherlands, the failed Armada against England, and expensive and fruitless interventions in France. But successful against the Turks with great naval victory at Lepanto in 1571. An obsessive bureaucrat and a devout Catholic. Built the great palace at the Escorial, where he died, leaving his empire divided, demoralized, and economically depressed.

Shakespeare, William (1564–1616): English dramatist and poet. Born in Stratford-upon-Avon, he came to London where he worked at The Globe theatre as actor and playwright. His 38 plays are written mostly in blank verse and include comedies such as *A Midsummer Night's Dream*; historical plays, including *Richard III* and *Henry V*; the Greek and Roman plays, which include *Julius Caesar* and *Antony and Cleopatra*; and the great tragedies, *Hamlet*, *Othello*, *Macbeth*, and *King Lear*. He also wrote more than 150 sonnets, published in 1609, which are of equal literary significance.

Titian, properly **Tiziano Vecellio** (c.1488–1576): the greatest of the Venetian painters. Painted many sensual and mythological works, including the *Venus of Urbino* (1538) and *Bacchus and Ariadne* (1523). He experimented with colour and revolutionized oil techniques. Has been described as the founder of modern painting, and had profound influence on later artists such as Tintoretto, Rubens, Velázquez, and Van Dyck.

Urban II (c.1035–99): Elected pope in 1088 during the schismatical pontificate of Guibert the antipope Clement III. He laid the emperor Henry IV of Germany under ban and drove him out of Italy, and triumphed similarly over Philip I of France. He inspired the First Crusade (1095–9).

Vesalius, Andreas (1514–64): Belgian anatomist, one of the first dissecters of human cadavers. Professor at Padua, Bologna, and Basle. Court physician to Emperor Charles V and Philip II of Spain. His great work *De Humani Corporis Fabrica* (1543) greatly advanced the science of biology with its excellent descriptions and drawings of bones and the nervous system, and repudiated Galenism. Sentenced to death by the Inquisition for "body snatching" and for dissecting the human body. Sentence commuted to a pilgrimage to Jerusalem; he died on the return journey.

William I (1027–87): Duke of Normandy, 1035–87, and king of England, 1066–87, known as "the Conqueror". Established control over the Duchy of Normandy through formidable fighting prowess. Promised the succession of the English throne, he defeated Harold Godwinson at Hastings in 1066, and secured kingdom with series of brutal campaigns, "harrying the North" in winter of 1069–70. Ordered compilation of the Domesday Book, produced in 1086. After 1072, visited England infrequently, dealing with rebellions in Normandy, where he was eventually killed.

William of Orange, known as **"the Silent"** (1533–84): Count of Nassau and Prince of Orange. A Roman Catholic with moderate and tolerant views. Took leading part in confederation of nobles calling for Philip II to relax heresy laws and suspend the Inquisition. Philip sent the hard-line Duke of Alva to be Regent in Netherlands. William withdrew to Germany, converted to Protestantism, and rallied army to liberate the Netherlands. Invaded in 1572, and through Pacification of Ghent (1576) and Union of Utrecht (1579), the northern provinces became the independent United Provinces. In 1584, the United Provinces formally renounced their allegiance to Spain, and William was assassinated at Delft by Balthasar Gérards.

Wycliffe, John (c.1330–84): English religious reformer. Criticized the wealth and power of the Church and upheld the Bible as the sole guide for doctrine. His teachings were disseminated throughout the country by itinerant preachers and are regarded as precursory to the Reformation. Instituted the first English translation of the complete Bible. His followers were known as Lollards.

Index

Picture Credits